Risk Management Intelligence

How to build an intelligence that manages an e-commerce service's risks on autopilot

Fabrice Colas, PhD

Fabrice Colas
Tel: +33 9 87 67 52 52
Email: rmi@fabricecolas.me

  https://www.linkedin.com/in/fabricecolas/
https://twitter.com/intent/user?user_id=2511334862

Third edition; first published in France in 2017

ISBN: 978-1979086950

To my parents

Contents

Contents

Contents

IV Big data and statistical learning to prevent fraud 109

11 Preliminary considerations for data analysis　　　111

12 Essential methods to measure risk and test hypotheses 123

13 Teaching machines to predict　　　139

V Towards risk management intelligence 155

14 Ideal fraud detection: The north star 157

15 Risk classification, escalation time, and rating 169

List of figures

List of tables

List of tables

List of tables

Preface

Where it stems from: The story

I once worked for a major online travel agent that sold two billion euros of airline tickets per year. The company had seen payment fraud spin out of control, and for several months it focused on reducing it by strengthening fraud prevention rules. Also, the company had just put together a team to configure the payment provider's fraud prevention system, verify payments, and manage chargebacks.

So the problem wasn't a lack of security or resources. The problem was also not a lack of reports or payment verifications. The problem was that the fraud prevention system had a poor design, reviewers had no decision support system, and data analyses lacked method and scale. They lacked the necessary software to *manage risk*.

When I joined the company, it was the peak season for selling airline tickets for summer travel. The VP of payments asked me to reduce the daily number of payment verifications. As the risk operation analysts could not review all the payments, part of the workload was absorbed by the customer service team.

In ten days, I retrieved a dataset of several million transactions from the payment provider, matched those with the fraud history, and identified several ineffective rules. Eliminating these rules reduced the workload. It was not a one-off chance achievement but the seed result of a *methodical process*, which I describe in this book.

Over the next four months, I developed automation, back tested, audited, and proposed changes, which allowed the company to halve the number of clients who were automatically rejected by the fraud prevention system while maintaining its payment fraud exposure. These changes saved the company tenths of millions of euros in revenue opportunities.

These bottom-line impacting results show that simply having a dedicated fraud prevention system is not enough, even with a team of statistical and risk operation analysts to manage the system and verify payments.

In addition to a fraud prevention system, it is also necessary to have a software for *risk management intelligence*. This software is not an additional operational cost. Instead, it's an investment that brings revenue to the company and benefits to the buyers.

The benefits of risk management intelligence

With *risk management intelligence*, the company is more likely to succeed in new markets, keep its risk exposure stable, and maximize its conversion.

It does not have to dedicate extra resources to fighting fraud in an emergency or to limit abruptly the range of payments accepted in an attempt to bring the fraud rate down.

It stays under the limits defined by the different card networks, thereby avoiding 2%[1] of its revenue from being charged back from one day, when it is still protected, to the other, when it is no longer protected.

Also, as fraud attempts are often repeated multiple times with a similar modus operandi, the company detects frauds and adapts its detection system more rapidly, which helps detect and stop similar fraud attempts at their onset, thereby reducing its fraud exposure.

Finally, preventing fraud in an emergency is more difficult and may lead to cost overruns, because the fraud detection system may not measure what's needed to screen the fraud out – it will take time before it is added, or because more expertise is necessary to deal with emergencies than is needed in properly planned situations.

The following table sums up these benefits.

---

[1]When the fraud rate of an e-commerce service exceeds some rates defined by the card schemes, a high-fraud-rate procedure is triggered; merchant accounts are closely watched by card schemes, and if their fraud rate does not decrease rapidly, they may lose their privilege to process cards from that card network.

Benefits of risk management intelligence
For the company as a whole and at transaction-level

Level	#	Benefits
Company	1	Prevent more than 2% of the sales revenue to transform as chargebacks.
	2	Do not abruptly limit the range of payments accepted to reduce fraud.
	3	Do not dedicate extra resources to fighting fraud in an emergency.
	4	Avoid the high-fraud-rate procedures of card schemes.
Transaction	5	Prevent repeat fraud offenses.
	6	Reduce required expertise-level.
	7	Reduce costs by properly scheduling training efforts and IT investments.

Why the way in which risks are managed is poor

Every day, many e-commerce services struggle when managing risk. They have to figure out ways to prevent risk themselves. They lack data, methods, and software to make the right decisions. This wastes so much time and leads to bad decisions.

Too often, risk operation analysts have to resort to intuition because they don't have access to the information they need. Frequently, executives have to explicitly demand audit reports by verbalizing their need, waiting for the reports to materialize, and making decisions. This process is slow and ineffective.

Analysts spend a lot of time making audit reports and showing information, but what is the basis of these reports? How much data are they based on? What can we conclude? Are the conclusions justified? Often, reports are developed inconsistently over time and based on limited data samples. They not only miss the big picture, they make it worse.

Should we blame the analysts who juggle different IT systems and need to justify their work to upper management? Maybe the wrong metrics are used to measure productivity and motivate.

We also blame the fraud detection software, but that is just one component. Usually, it's possible to build something on top of what exists with no additional software. The massive results I saw with the online travel agent prove this is feasible.

In addition, the expected benefits of *risk management intelligence* are consistently underestimated, probably because it's new for most businesses—usually, it's reserved for financial institutions or very big companies. This is a shame because brilliant methods and software exist to automate repetitive tasks and improve the accuracy of the decisions we make when it comes to risk.

To add to the problem, although everyone knows what a chargeback or fraud is, how to call a customer to confirm an order, or what a blacklist is, few know what a risk is, how it's calculated, and how to translate it back to the e-commerce service.

This book provides answers to these questions and more, as we'll discuss in the next section.

What you will get from this book

This book will help you grasp the global picture, go deep into the details, and name the different elements and methods used in risk management intelligence and fraud detection systems.

Part I will review online payment processing when things work correctly. It will picture the current landscape of payment methods, why they exist, and where they come from; describe the different intermediaries involved in an online payment; and review the three stages of online payments, i.e., setting up the necessary conditions, exchanging the counterparty, and fulfilling the order.

Part II will help you understand what happens when payment fraud occurs and things go wrong. It will describe the reasons why things go wrong, e.g., because payment intermediaries have failed to guarantee trust and fraudsters search for arbitrage opportunities; review how things go wrong; and examine who is vulnerable to fraud.

Part III will present how to prevent payment fraud and make it work. It will provide a landscape of the existing solutions and help you choose one strategy. It will offer you a bird's-eye view of a typical fraud prevention process, dive into the bits and pieces of developing a fraud prevention system, and review how to build a feedback loop to audit the system.

Part IV will help you understand how big data, artificial intelligence, and machine learning work in relation to fraud prevention. It will provide preliminary considerations to think about before analyzing data, describe a set of essential methods to measure risk and test hypotheses, and examine how to teach machines to predict.

Finally, part V is the keystone of this book. It focuses on how to better manage risk. It will discuss the ideal fraud detection system, provide a classification of risks, define escalation time, recall the concept of ratings, and show how risk can be piloted in e-commerce services with value at risk (VAR).

Throughout the book, you will learn many of the methods that fraud prevention and *risk management intelligence* use. By the end, you will also have a clear picture of the internal components of the present and future risk management systems for e-commerce services.

How to save time implementing these ideas

After reading this book, you may wish to change the way your e-commerce service manages risk or apply some of the ideas presented. For help with this, you can contact us.

 rmi@fabricecolas.me

+33 9 87 67 52 52

https://www.linkedin.com/in/fabricecolas/

We provide on-site training in France and abroad. We offer our expert advice regarding your systems or management of risk. We have a software as a service offering and provide support.

Final thoughts

It doesn't matter if you are an investor or a CEO, CFO, VP of payment, payment fraud manager, statistical or risk operation analyst, HR consultant, lawyer, or compliance officer—everyone who deals with e-commerce services needs to have some understanding, either in-depth or general, of online payment processing, fraud, fraud detection, machine learning, and risk management.

The process components and methods are relevant to all levels of seniority in the business. They're not just for those who carry out payment verifications or make audit reports. They're also relevant to those who need to understand the terms being used and a vision of the whole process, such as executives, lawyers, or investors.

I Online payments: When things just work

Background

Paying depends on the concept of *ownership* and *property*, which can be private, collective, or common and which can be gained, transferred, or lost [111, 12].

A payment is a means of transferring ownership of a product or service to another person, e.g., a notional value in a given currency of exchange, such as euros, pounds, or dollars.

Systems called *payment methods* exist to facilitate money exchanges between parties. In particular, if parties:

- do not trust each other;

- do not know each other;

- are geographically distant;

- speak different languages; or

- use different money systems or currencies.

The terms of use for each payment method are primarily determined by legal regulations and, in many cases, by industry standards and private companies, which may themselves provide and organize those payments methods. Examples of payment methods include cash, checks, payment cards, the email, the phone, blockchains, etc.

To facilitate and secure payments from a giver to a receiver, a number of intermediaries exist. The role of these intermediaries is to help settle payments, make it easier to pay, and improve the cost-effectiveness and reliability of payments.

Problem

Given the diversity of the many regulations, payment methods, intermediaries, and payment scenarios available, how are payments *engineered* and *orchestrated*?

This is what we will look at in this part.

Outline

First, we will review some of the payment methods used to pay for items online today. Then, we will investigate the different entities that carry out payments online; this is what we call passing the witness. Finally, we will describe the three steps required for online payments.

1   Payment methods: The past, present, and future

Background   A galaxy of payment methods exists when processing online payments. This diversity results from the conversion of traditional payment methods, like checks and credit cards, to online payments made using the Internet. However, after two decades of Internet use, a new set of payment methods is under development.

Problem   What range of payment methods is available to clients when making online purchases on e-commerce services?

1.1 Checks, i.e., the traditional bill of exchange

Checks are the traditional way of transferring money from a drawer, i.e., the person writing the check, to the beneficiary, i.e., the person whose name is written on the check. In other words, a check is a financial instrument or a type of bill of exchange.

Checks used to be a highly popular non-cash payment method, but their usage has fallen due to the rise of electronic payments, which is what the following figure illustrates. Because checks are still used online when ordering expensive products, we mention them as part of our online payment processing review.

Checks are still used
30% less in 7 years in France

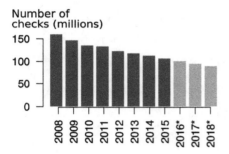

Sources: the data series covers 2008 to 2015 and is taken from the Verifiance service provider in France [48], which allows retailers to test checks against a national database of bad or opposed checks [88]; 2016, 2017, and 2018 are estimates.

1.2 Payment cards, i.e., plastic cards used digitally

Various types of payment cards exist, such as:

- major cards;

- regional cards;

- specialty cards; and

- cards with some stored value.

Amongst these different card subtypes, we then distinguish between *debit* and *credit cards*.

Debit cards   When a payment is made, funds are directly transferred from the client's bank account.

Credit cards   The merchant is paid with money borrowed from the issuing bank that granted a line of credit to the cardholder.

The major card schemes include:

- American Express (AMEX), which was created in 1850 [54];

- Diners Club International, which was created in 1950 and was the first independent credit card company in the world [84];

- Visa which was created in 1958 [132]; and

- MasterCard, which was created in 1966 [101].

Regional cards include:

- Carte Bleue, which was created in 1967 in France [62];

- Bancomat, which was created in 1983 in Italy [57]; and

- Girocard, which was created in 1991 in Germany [93].

Carte Bleue, Bancomat, and Girocard are three examples of

national interbank ATM networks. To work abroad, Carte Bleue cards are usually co-branded with Visa. Most Bancomat cards are also co-branded with MasterCard's Maestro service or Visa's debit or V Pay service, whereas Girocard are usually co-branded with MasterCard's Maestro or Visa's V Pay.

UnionPay [66], which was created in 2002 in China, is the largest card payment organization in the world, ahead of Visa and MasterCard. It provides bank cards in mainland China and the only interbank network that links ATMs and banks in China.

Finally, RuPay [121], which was created in 2012 in India, is an Indian domestic card scheme launched in 2012. It competes with MasterCard and Visa in India to facilitate payments at all Indian banks and financial institutions.

1.3 Coupons, i.e., the pre-sale's incentive for buyers

Traditionally, a coupon is a ticket that can be used to get a rebate on the purchase of a product. Coupons have several objectives, some of those are reported in the following table.

Objectives of coupons
To offer a discount to price-conscious consumers

1	Reduce the price of an item.
2	Provide a free sample.
3	Help track the customer demographics.

Sources: [73]

In online payment processing, coupons are referred to as coupon codes, promotional codes, promo codes, discount vouchers, or referral codes. They offer a discount to *price-conscious* consumers who, in the absence of a coupon, might go shop elsewhere.

Various types of coupons exist. The main ones are, of course, traditional discount and free shipping coupons, but other types of coupons offer a free item each time one item is bought. Some coupons help promote free trials, whereas others are seasonal, e.g., they work when a product is launched or during the rebate season.

1.4 Direct debit and online banking, i.e., the pure players

Direct debit is a payment mechanism in which one person withdraws money from another person's bank account directly. The person may be an individual or a business. In this scenario, the payer and payee agree and pre-authorize future debits; however, the date on which the funds are withdrawn and the amount are not yet defined. Typically, direct debit is used for recurring payments.

The payer has the ability to cancel the authorization at any time, but the issuing bank can also cancel an order if it breaches the terms of the bank account, e.g., if there is an overdraft.

Direct debit is available in many countries around the world, such as the United States, with an automated clearing house (ACH) [56]; the United Kingdom, where more than 70% of all household bills are paid with direct debit; the Netherlands, where more than 50% of all online banking transactions are made with direct debit; and also Germany, Spain, Brazil, and South Africa.

Notably, there is an e-commerce payment system called iDeal in the Netherlands [95]; it is low cost and virtually risk free for merchants because it carries no risk of payment fraud. Customers use the same website they use for their online banking to perform the following tasks:

1. authenticate themselves;

2. validate the availability of funds in their account;

3. provide a guarantee from their bank that the payment will be made;

4. push the payment to the merchant (instead of pulling it); and

5. debit the client's account directly with no use of a third-party account.

All major Dutch banks participate in iDeal, including ABN Amro, ING Bank, and Rabobank.

1.5 Single Euro Payments Area (SEPA)

The goal of SEPA [122] is to simplify payment integration within Europe. SEPA allows customers to make payments in euros to anyone in the eurozone using a single account and set of instruments. It has three types of financial instruments:

1. the *SEPA credit transfer*, which aims to facilitate payment initiation, processing, and reconciliation;

2. the *SEPA direct debit*, which involves requesting money from someone else, with prior approval, and crediting it to oneself (this is an example of a pull payment);

3. the *SEPA card framework*, which aims to be a set of consistent principles and rules to deliver a consistent user experience to merchants and cardholders.

By standardizing payment processing, SEPA enables economies of scale in Europe. The following table summarizes the four types of economies of scale brought by the SEPA framework.

Benefits of the Single Euro Payment Area

Standardize payment processing and bring economies of scale

#	Benefit
1	Financial instruments
2	Standards
3	Procedures
4	Strategies

1.6 Cryptocurrencies, i.e., the possible future of payment

Cryptocurrencies like bitcoins, litecoins, or peercoins are digital assets that people can exchange using cryptography to secure transactions. Today, several hundred digital currencies exist; today's major cryptocurrencies are summarized in the following table.

Major cryptocurrencies

100,000 merchants worldwide accept bitcoins

Name	Date	Merchant acceptance	Symbol	Total
Bitcoins	2009	100,000	XBT	21M
Litecoins	2011	-	LTC	84M
Peercoins	2012	-	PPC	Unlimited

Sources: Bitcoin [60], Litecoin [100], Peercoin [113]

Cryptocurrencies have three main benefits. Their ledger is not centralized but *community-maintained*. They are *less prone to chargebacks* than payment cards. And they are a *push*-type payment method. We detail these three benefits in the following paragraphs.

Community-maintained ledger
The timestamping schemes allows the community to maintain the ledger without a third party. The safety, integrity, and balance of the ledger is maintained by the community assuming that the ledger is maintained honestly.

Less prone to chargeback
Cryptocurrencies are not as vulnerable to chargebacks as credit cards are because the sender cannot counterfeit or reverse cryptocurrencies arbitrarily.

Push payment
Cryptocurrencies are push payments, which means that the cryptocurrency holder sends the right amount to the merchant.

In terms of acceptance, some major online retailers, such as Overstock, Expedia, Newegg, and Shopify stores, accept bitcoins as currency. However, new payment service providers are accepting cryptocurrencies too. Finally, various points of sales (POS) also exist on smartphones, such as Coinbase [67] and Coinify [68], or on terminals, such as Coinkite [69].

1.7 Payment methods: Key points

In brief

The historical and current landscape of online payment methods is composed of checks, which are the traditional bill of exchange; coupons, which are pre-sale incentives for buyers; and payment cards, which are plastic cards that can be used online.

Current and future payment methods are direct debit and online banking, which can be used to pay online; the Single Euro Payments Area (SEPA), which is a framework that brings economies of scale to Europe when processing payments; and cryptocurrencies, which are likely to play an important role in the future online payment landscape.

Key points

- The present landscape of payment methods has methods that existed before the Internet and that have been adapted for use online, and other methods that only exist through the Internet.

- Many of the available payment method options depend on industrial partnerships and country-specific initiatives.

- The SEPA framework aims to unify the European market of payment processing.

- The stability of payment industry partnerships in each country, the fact that checks are still in use today, and the adaptation of payment cards for online use exemplify the stickiness of choices related to payment.

2 | Online payment: Passing the witness

Background In previous chapter we introduced a number of *payment methods*, which are systems designed to facilitate money exchange between parties who don't trust each other or who can't exchange money easily because of distance, language, or currency. Exchanging money between a *giver* and a *receiver* is a process that involves several intermediaries.

Some of those intermediaries are on the side of the giver, which sends the money. Others are on the side of the receiver, which receives the money. Additional intermediaries act as referees and make sure that the right amount of money is transfered.

Problem In an online payment processing scenario, what are the different roles and responsibilities of each intermediary?

2.1 Issuing side, i.e., the giving side

The issuing side comprises the cardholder and the issuing bank. The issuer issues payments on behalf of its customers when cardholders use branded payment cards to make purchases online.

In this context, the payment is called an outbound transfer. Outbound fund transfers may be realized from the client's bank account, lines of credit, or credit cards. If the cardholder cannot pay off his or her debts, the issuing bank is liable for them.

In the following table we describe the top-5 debit card issuers per country for the United States of America, China, India, United Kingdom, and France.

2.2 Acquiring side, i.e., the receiving side

The acquiring side comprises the merchant and the acquirer. The role of the acquirer is to process credit or debit card payments on behalf of the merchant.

To do so, the acquirer may create a merchant account and open a corresponding line of credit; however, a merchant account with a line of credit is not always created; for example, it is not mandatory with Stripe and PayPal.

Under this agreement, the acquirers pay the merchant for the pay-

Top debit card issuers in the world

In purchase volume, Chinese issuers trust the top-4

	United States	China	India	UK	France
1	Bank of America	Agricultural Bank	HDFC Bank Ltd.	Lloyds	Crédit Agricole
2	Wells Fargo	ICBC	ICICI Bank Ltd.	RBS NatWest	Crédit Mutuel
3	JP Morgan Chase	Bank of China	State Bank of India	Barclays	La Banque Postale
4	PNC	Bank of Commun.	Citibank	HSBC	BPCE
5	US Bank	China Merchants	Axis Bank Ltd.	Santander Cards	

Sources: United States, China, UK and France [37], India [29]

ments received daily. This payment breaks down as follows:

$$\begin{aligned} &\text{Gross sales} \\ &- \text{Reversals} \\ &- \text{Interchange fees} \\ &= \textbf{Daily payments} \end{aligned} \qquad (2.1)$$

In the following, we describe the *gross sales*, *reversals*, and *interchange fees*, which determine merchant's *daily payments*.

Gross sales   It corresponds to the total sales value for merchandise sold through the e-commerce site or marketplace, for the set of payment methods offered by the e-commerce service, and the set of countries in which the merchant operates.

Reversals   Reversals or chargebacks correspond to a payment processing mechanism to return funds to the client.

There are two types of reversals: those that comply with the sales term and are legitimate and those that are due to payment fraud.

Interchange fees   It corresponds to the amount acquiring banks pay for the privilege of accepting card-based transactions.

The total interchange fee is the sum of the individual transaction fees charged by the card issuer, the card network, the acquirer, and the merchant's own bank [4]; in practice, there are about 300 interchange fees [26, 11].

Finally, the acquiring bank charges the merchant acquirer fees.

In the table below we list the *top-5 acquirers per country* in the United States of America, China, India, United Kingdom and France. Notably, we remark that none of the top acquirers overlap across these major countries, which illustrates that the largest acquiring services of the world dominate their domestic market, first.

Top acquirers per country
Top acquiring services do not overlap across countries

	United States	China	India	UK	France
1	FirstData	Alipay	SBI	Worldpay	Crédit Mutuel
2	Vantiv	ICBC	HDFC Bank	Barclays	Crédit Agricole
3	JP Morgan	China UMS	Axis Bank	Global Payments	BPCE
4	Bank of America	Minsheng Bank	ICICI Bank	Lloyds CMS.	BNP Paribas
5	Heartland	CUP Guangzhou	RBI		Société Générale

Sources: United States [35], China [24], India [21], UK and France [36]

2.3 Card schemes, i.e., the referees

Card schemes, which are also referred to as card networks, are payment networks that manage brands of payment cards. Some examples of credit card schemes are Visa, MasterCard, Discover, American Express, Diners Club, and Japan Credit Bureau (JCB).

By becoming a member, financial institutions such as issuing and acquiring banks receive the privilege of processing payments using the network of that card scheme [61].

There are basically two types of card schemes: a *three-party* scheme or closed scheme; and a *four-party* scheme or open scheme.

| **Three-party schemes** | With these schemes (e.g., Diners Club, Discover Card, and American Express), there is no charge between the issuer and acquirer. This is the incentive for this type of card scheme. |
| **Four-party schemes** | On the other hand, in the four-party scheme, such as that offered by Visa, MasterCard, UnionPay, JCB, and RuPay, the card network acts as a router between the issuer and the acquirer. There is a so-called *interchange fee*. |

In the following table we report the major *card schemes* (or *card networks*) of the world. We remark that:

1. the oldest card scheme company is American Express;

2. the major card schemes are from the United States of America;

3. there are two billions cardholders worldwide; and

4. three-party schemes are smaller than four-party schemes.

Major card schemes
More than 2 billion cardholders worldwide

Card scheme	Date	Empl.	Country	Card-holders	Party 3	4
Visa	1958	11,300	United States	* 883M		
MasterCard	1966	10,300	United States	* 720M		
UnionPay	2002	-	China	* 330M		
JCB	1961	2,700	Japan	* 79M		
RuPay	2012	-	India	25M		
Discover	1985	15,000	United States	44M		
Diners Club	1950			* 6M		
American Express	1850	54,000	United States	110M		

Sources: Visa [132, 43], MasterCard [101, 43], UnionPay [66, 43], JSB [98, 43], RuPay [121], Discover [85, 13], Diners Club [84, 43], American Express [54]; figures with a * are from 2012 [43]

2.4 PayPal, i.e., the troublemaker

PayPal, which was created in 1998, is one of the largest online payment company of the world. It allows individuals and businesses to send, receive, and hold funds in many currencies worldwide.

In online payment processing, PayPal is sometimes referred to as *the troublemaker*, because it differs from the acquiring and issuing payment mechanism presented above. Clients just attach payment methods to their accounts, e.g., a payment card or a bank account, and then they use their PayPal account to make payments online.

Hence, PayPal could be regarded as both an issuer and acquirer in terms of roles, although the acquiring and issuing bank still exist underneath. Instead, PayPal is a new intermediary that greatly simplified how money is transferred when processing payments online.

The following table summarizes the main characteristics of PayPal. Notably, we remark that the number of active users of PayPal is proportional to the number of cardholders of the largest card networks of the world, i.e., Visa and MasterCard.

PayPal
196 million active users in 2016

Company	Date	Empl.	Country	Active users
PayPal	1998	18,000	United States	197M

Sources: [112, 44]

2.5 Settling payments, i.e., getting things right

Issuing and acquiring banks need to maintain cash accounts to clear the payment obligations associated with their daily transactions.

In some instances, acquirers and issuers can settle their payments directly; these are referred to as *interbank settlements*. However, issuing and acquiring banks depend on *settlement bank services* in the absence of bilateral agreements.

In the following we describe what *interbank settlements* and *settlement bank services* are.

Interbank settlements   They occur when acquiring and issuing banks come to a *bilateral* agreement.   These direct agreements permit fund transfers that are almost as inexpensive as balance transfers within a single bank.

Settlement bank services   Designated by credit card unions to facilitate transaction settlements, they receive funds from the issuer, which debits the account of the credit card holder, and transfer those funds back to the acquirer, which credits the merchant's account.

Though, note that the term "settlement bank" is misleading because institutions providing such settlement services are not necessarily banks; for example, Visa and MasterCard both provide such a service.

2.6 Online payment: Key points

In brief

Online payment processing relies on the concept of a giver and a receiver. The giving side is composed of the account owner or cardholder, while the cardholder's bank is called the issuer or issuing bank. The receiving side is composed of the merchant; the merchant's bank, which is called the acquirer or acquiring bank; and the company that acquires payments, which is called either the payment service provider or the acquiring bank.

If a payment is made using a card, there are also card schemes or networks that define the rules used to process card payments as well as companies called settling banks that are in charge of settling the payments.

Key points

- Orchestrating online payments requires clearly defined roles and rules; many of these rules are defined by card networks.

- China has the biggest issuers and acquirers in the world.

- The top acquirers are country specific and do not overlap.

- PayPal has hacked the established order; its number of active users is similar to the number of cardholders in the largest card networks.

- Approximately seven entities are needed to process online payments from payment cards; these are summarized in the following table.

Payment processing intermediaries

Seven entities are involved to process online payments

Side	Intermediary	#	Role
Issuing side	Cardholder	1	The online buyer
	Issuing bank	2	The cardholder's bank
Acquiring side	Merchant	3	The e-commerce service
	Acquiring bank	4	The merchant's bank
	Acquiring service	5	A payment service provider or the merchant's bank
Referee	Card networks	6	The companies that define the rules used to process payments
Facilitator	Settling bank	7	The company that helps transfer the money

3   Payment process: Three steps to online ordering

Background   When considering the payment process in its entirety, a sequence of steps must be carried out before a payment can occur and be considered successful. Once the conditions for payments to occur are ready, most of those steps are fully automated, and online payments are completed within a few seconds.

Problem   What are the conditions for online payments to occur? How is the counterparty exchanged? What happens after the payment has been made? In this chapter we will address these questions.

3.1 Step #1: Setting up the necessary conditions

First, the consumer and issuing bank enter a contract that defines the acceptable use for the payment card. Among other things, the contract defines:

- the geographical usage limits, e.g., national or international;

- the maximum withdrawal amount; and

- the period, e.g., a seven-day or 30-day rolling basis.

Once both parties sign the contract, the issuer requests that the card be printed by a payment card manufacturer. A list of the biggest manufacturers in the world is reported in the following table.

Biggest payment card manufacturers
Top-5 manufacturers have made 3 billion payment cards

Company	Date	Country	Empl.	Cards (Millions)		
				Magn.	Chip	Total
Gemalto	1998	France	14,000	151	729	880
Perfect Plastic	1965	United States	10,400	602	10	612
Oberthur Technologies	1984	France	6,300	176	364	540
Giesecke & Devrient	1852	United States	11,400	139	361	500
CPI	1995	United States	1,250	313	74	387

Sources: payment card characteristics [34, 89, 114, 109, 92, 30]; list of payment card manufacturers available at the International Card Manufacturers Association (ICMA).

Payment cards are usually *delivered* in one of two ways. The first option is to send the card *directly* to the client; the second option is to make it available at one of the *bank agencies*. For security reasons, the PIN code and the card are usually sent in two different envelopes.

Once the cardholder receives the card, activation frequently requires an initial debit transaction from an ATM. Then, cardholders can use the payment cards in two ways, when the *card is present* (CP), and when the *card is not present* (CNP).

Card present and card not present
Merchant can see the card (in a shop) or not (online)

Type	Description
CP	Cardholder uses the card to pay in a brick-and-mortar shop using a point of sale (POS) or terminal.
CNP	Cardholders buy online with their payment card. It is *card not present* because the online merchant does not see the card.

Aside from payments made with cards, there are also electronic ways to transfer money as mentioned previously, e.g., via direct debit, SEPA, IBAN, or wire transfers.

More generally, payments are either *push* or *pull*, which is what we summarize in the following table.

Push and pull payments
Clients authorize merchants to pull money, or they push it

Type	Initiator	Description
Push	Client	Client pushes the money to the merchant.
Pull	Merchant	Merchant pulls money from client's account; to do so it requires prior authorization from client.

3.2 Step #2: Exchanging the counterparty

Once clients finish shopping online, they select the payment methods they will use. Major payment methods are usually accepted, e.g., MasterCard or Visa, and PayPal.

Some bank transfer options are usually available, e.g., wire transfers or IBAN. E-commerce services tend to accept checks too, and depending on the geographical location, they may accept online banking payment methods, e.g., Giropay, iDeal, and Sofort.

At that point, the e-commerce services can use their *bank's acquiring service* or use a *payment service provider*.

Bank's acquiring service	In this case, the merchant's bank provides the acquiring services. It offers the range of payment methods that corresponds to the merchant needs.
Payment service provider	Alternatively, the merchant's bank does not provide the range of payment methods the merchant needs.
	Therefore, the merchant enters a contract with a dedicated *payment service provided* (PSP). PSPs tend to provide a broader range of payment methods both locally and internationally than merchant banks.

Whether the merchant uses the acquiring services of his bank or of a payment service provider, it will have to comply with the rules of a *contract*. Notably, some of the contract rules define what happens when a chargeback occurs and who is *liable*, because not all payment methods bear the same payment risk.

In practice, online banking payments and bank transfers tend to be safe, whereas payments made with credit or debit cards are exposed to payment fraud and, sometimes, to *chargebacks*. A chargeback is the reversal of a payment.

3.3 Step #3: Fulfilling the order

Depending on its exposure to payment fraud, the e-commerce service may *ship directly* the product or run *fraud detection* first and *then ship*. The table below summarizes these two options and the reasons that may lead to each.

Shipment decision
If there is a payment risk, order fulfillment is delayed

Direct shipping	Reason
Yes	If there is no payment risk, products or services are shipped right away.
No	A series of tests to reduce payment risk, are carried out before shipment.

In the case the e-commerce service carries out fraud detection, it may perform two types of detections to reduce its risk of payment fraud: *fully automated detection* and *manual detection*. Later in this book, we will discuss both strategies.

However, another step exists: *chargeback management*. When the e-commerce service receives a chargeback for which it is liable, the merchant analyzes the chargeback request. It may *accept* the request or *defend* it.

Finally, while most payment methods are almost *immediate*, like those made with Visa, MasterCard, American Express, PayPal, or online banking payment methods (e.g., Sofort, iDeal), some are not, i.e., payments made with checks or bank transfers (e.g., IBAN, Wire). In such cases, the merchant waits for the payment before preparing the shipment.

3.4 Payment process: Key points

In brief

The necessary conditions to enable cardholders to pay online are signing a contract between the cardholder and the issuer and manufacturing, delivering, and activating the payment card.

An online payment is the process of exchanging a counterparty between a cardholder and a merchant; most of the steps are fully automated and are carried out within a few seconds.

After the exchange of the counterparty, the merchant fulfills the order by shipping the product or providing the service to the client.

Key points

- Payments made in brick-and-mortar shops are called *card present* (CP) payments, and payments made online are called *card not present* (CNP) payments.

- If the cardholder authorizes and pays the merchant directly from his or her bank account, the payment is called a *push* payment, but if the merchant starts the payment, the payment is called a *pull* payment.

- Online payment acquisition is done by the merchant's bank or by a dedicated company called a *payment service provider*.

- After exchanging the counterparty, a merchant may *directly ship* the product or *verify the payment* and *then ship* the item.

II   Payment fraud: When things go wrong

Background

In the previous part, we reviewed the foundation for payments between people who may not know each other, who may use different currencies, or who may be geographically distant.

We described several payment methods that exist to facilitate payments; these include checks, payment cards, the email, the phone, and blockchains. Then we briefly introduced the intermediaries that exist to orchestrate payments and make them successful.

Payments by card involve the cardholder; the issuing bank, which is the cardholder's bank; the card schemes, which grant issuing banks the right to print payment cards with their brands; the merchant; the merchant's bank; the acquiring service; and, sometimes, a settling bank.

The role of these intermediaries is to make payments easy, reliable, and cost-effective for the givers, i.e., the cardholders, and the receivers, i.e., the merchants.

Finally, we reviewed the three-step process to make a payment, i.e., establish the necessary conditions for a payment to occur, exchange the counter-party, and fulfill the payment.

Problem

Although the online payment process goes *right* most of the time, in some scenarios it *fails*. Some reasons why a payment may fail are legitimate, but others are not. In this part, we describe what happens when things go wrong, particularly when payment fraud occurs.

Outline

We first look at why things may go wrong when processing online payments. Then we discuss how things go wrong, i.e., the processes used to commit payment fraud. Finally, we identify the factors that influence payment fraud.

4 | Why things go wrong

Background When payers and payees initiate a payment, each one builds expectations. The payee expects the notional amount to be credited to its bank account, and the payer expects to receive a product or service as described by the payee.

The expectation levels of the payer and the payee are partly determined by *legal obligations* and partly by the *market*, which sets the standard for how payments and orders are usually fulfilled.

Problem Although payments are successful in most cases, in some instances they are not. In this chapter, we review *why things may go wrong* when paying online.

4.1 Online payment as high-trust communications

Payments are high-trust communications in which two people exchange money. Sometimes, money exchanges occur directly between a payer and a payee, and the sale concludes when the two parties agree on a price and a currency.

However, physically exchanging the money is not always possible. In the table below we summarize some of the factors that hinder payment.

Limits to the exchange of money

Physically exchanging money is not always possible

#	Payer and payee
1	Do not know each other.
2	Do not trust each other.
3	Are limited by the volume amount to exchange—too high.
4	Are limited by the speed of the transaction—too slow.
5	Are in different locations.
6	Use different currencies.
7	Speak different languages.

Hence, the roles of intermediaries are to make it possible for payers and payees to exchange money and to build the necessary *trust* to conclude the payment.

4.2 From arbitrage opportunities to payment fraud

When intermediaries fail to guarantee 100% trust, there is room for payment fraud. The ways in which businesses are exposed to payment fraud depend on *arbitrage*. Below we define the *arbitrage process*.

The arbitrage process
To exploit price differences between markets

> Arbitrage is the process of buying a product or service on a first market, and reselling it on a second market at a greater price.

A necessary condition for a commercial transaction to be *profitable* is the existence of an arbitrage opportunity. However, the same holds for frauds, where an arbitrage opportunity is also necessary for frauds to occur.

With payment fraud, the opportunity is to buy products or services with a stolen payment card, or with card informations bought on the blackmarket but at a reduced cost. In turn, the greater the arbitrage opportunity, the higher the *exposure* to payment fraud— in a later chapter, we will define more precisely the term exposure.

Instances of domains with large *arbitrage opportunities* are:

- insurance companies (e.g., claims);

- rental companies (e.g., car rental, AirBnB);

- job applications; and

- e-commerce transactions.

4.3 Legitimate and illegitimate payment reversals

Previously, we described payments as a communication between a payer and a payee, which is made possible by payment intermediaries. Most of the time, payments are *successful*.

However, sometimes they are not, notably if payment intermediaries could not guarantee the needed trust, or if fraudsters exploited arbitrage opportunities between the blackmarket and the real market.

More generally, there are two reasons for payment reversals, i.e., chargebacks: *legitimate* and *illegitimate* ones. In the following paragraphs, we examine each reason type.

Legitimate reversals	A chargeback is *legitimate* when a payment is reversed after both the client and merchant agree on the reversal.
	Instances of legitimate reversals are when a client changes his mind, when a client returns a faulty product, or when the products were damaged during delivery.
Illegitimate reversals	On the other hand, a chargeback is *illegitimate* when the card is used fraudulently.

It may happen if the client was victim of *phishing* or *social engineering* , or if a payment intermediary that processed his card was victim of a major *data leak.* We will go into more details in a later chapter on these reasons.

The following table summarizes some of the reasons why payments reversals happen.

Payment reversal reasons
Reasons are either legitimate or illegitimate

Reasons	#	Description
Legitimate	1	Delivered products are damaged.
	2	Products never arrive.
	3	Products are out of stock.
	4	Customer changes his mind.
Illegitimate	5	Payment card used fraudulently, e.g., after a data leak, phishing, or social engineering.

In each case, the terms of the sale, the merchants' policies, and legal regulations define whether the payment will be reimbursed totally or partially or if products will be redelivered.

The payment conditions, such as whether the payment was verified using 3D Secure, will determine who is *liable*: the *issuer* or the *merchant* when a chargeback is due to payment fraud. Below we describe who is liable in case of chargeback.

Issuer is liable   In most situations, the issuer takes the loss.

Merchant is liable	The only reason why a merchant would be liable for online purchases is that it does not process payments to the most secure standard, e.g., by disabling 3D Secure for online payments—which is the merchant's choice[1].

4.4 Why things go wrong: Key points

In brief

Trust is a necessary component for a payment to occur between the payer and payee, which also justifies the existence of payment processing intermediaries whose role is in part to *establish* and *guarantee trust*.

Arbitrage opportunities involve the process of acquiring a product somewhere and reselling it elsewhere at a greater price. An arbitrage opportunity is needed for payment fraud to occur.

There are two broad categories of payment failure reasons: *legitimate* and *illegitimate*. Illegitimate reasons are those that correspond to payment fraud.

Key points

- *Trust* is needed for payments to occur.

- Payment industry *intermediaries* help establish this trust.

- Exploiting price differences between markets is *arbitrage*.

---

[1]If 3D Secure helps secure payment, there are some reasons, notably economical, why merchants disable it. The loss in conversion and the lower checkout velocity are two of these reasons.

- Fraud may happen if there are *arbitrage opportunities*.

- In case of fraud, issuers are liable if the payment is made with 3D Secure; merchants are liable if 3D Secure is disabled.

5   How things go wrong

Background   In the previous chapter, we described why things may go wrong when processing online payments. Some of the reasons are legitimate, and others are not.

Credit card fraud is an illegitimate payment failure reason. It may occur after the card details have been shared and the card has been used without the cardholder's authorization.

This may be the case if the card is shared or accessible within a family or at the cardholder's work. However, this may also be the case if hackers intercept the card information, e.g., via a data leak, phishing, or social engineering .

Problem   What is the source of credit card fraud? How does it materialize? What happens after it occurs? We will review these questions in this chapter.

5.1 Data leaks

Data leaks (or data breaches) occur when hackers penetrate the IT systems of companies that process payments. Once the hackers get into these IT systems, they can intercept information such as credit card numbers.

In 2014, a massive data leak of private and business clients occurred at JP Morgan Chase; clients' details were accessed, but their credit card information was not. Earlier in 2013, Target was hacked; in that case, credit card information was leaked. The table below lists some of the largest data breaches in recent years.

Largest data breaches
Black market flooded with sensitive information

Company	Date	Number and type of records	
Yahoo	2013	1,000,000,000	Account information
JP Morgan Chase	2014	76,000,000	Names, addresses, phone numbers, emails
Target	2014	70,000,000	Credit card information
Home Depot	2014	56,000,000	Credit card information
Weebly	2016	43,000,000	Account credentials

Sources: Yahoo [133]; JP Morgan Chase [46, 39]; Target [126, 6, 33]; Home Depot [32]; Weebly [45]; list of data breaches [99]; visual representation of data breaches [22]

5.2 Phishing

Phishing [115] is another technique used to intercept credit card information. It involves sending emails or building websites that look like they are from real companies but are not.

Victims follow links from emails, enter their credit card information, and in some cases, are even redirected to the spoofed company so the phishing looks innocuous.

5.3 Social engineering

Social engineering [123] involves the practice of impersonating other people to obtain confidential information, such as credit card details.

Those who commit social engineering collect data on their victims, e.g., date of birth, home address, or email address. They find answers to security questions and obtain the information needed to make fraudulent purchases.

5.4 After card details have leaked

Once the card details leak, the real cardholder and issuer may learn about the data leak, i.e., be *aware*, or they may not, i.e., be *unaware*.

Data breach aware	If they learn about the leak, the primary option is to cancel the card and reprint it. However, if details leak for too many cards, this may not be economically or logistically feasible because it would take too much time to reprint, ship, and activate all the new cards.

In that case, the issuing bank may temporarily or permanently take additional security measures to protect its cardholders.

Data breach unaware If neither the issuer nor the cardholder learn about the leak, the cardholder will be *vulnerable* to credit card fraud.

Fraud may occur when the hacker who obtained the credit card details uses them to buy online services or products or, more likely, after fraudsters buy the credit card information on the black market and then purchase services or products online.

Finally, so-called mules [105] are sometimes used to pick up goods that are bought online.

5.5 How things go wrong: Key points

In brief

In recent years, major *data leaks* have flooded the black market with account and credit card information, which fraudsters can use to carry out fraud.

Hackers may also collect sensitive information by mirroring websites and intercepting credentials used to log in to those services; this is known as *phishing*.

Alternatively, once hackers have some information about their target, they may use *social engineering*, e.g., the technique of impersonating someone over the phone or via email, and answering security questions to obtain sensitive information.

Key points

- Highly *sensitive information* travels through or is stored at merchants, banks, and online service providers.

- This sensitive information, such as credit card numbers or account credentials, can be resold on the *black market*.

- *Hacking, phishing,* and *social engineering* are three ways in which sensitive information may leak to the black market.

- Once data has leaked, victims are *vulnerable to fraud*.

- Protecting vulnerable clients requires *security measures*. The selection of these measures is influenced by their total costs.

6 Who is vulnerable to payment fraud

Background   In previous chapters, we reviewed why payment may fail and described payment fraud as an illegitimate payment failure reason. Then we reviewed how credit card fraud materializes. Now we focus on identifying the *e-commerce services the most vulnerable* to payment fraud.

When processing payments online, e-merchants, issuers, acquirers, payment gateways, card schemes and, eventually, settling banks may be impacted by credit card fraud. Depending on each type of payment, the interests may differ.

In particular, if the payment is 3D Secure-enabled [49], the burden of the fraud shifts from the acquiring side to the issuing side.

Moreover, we distinguish two subtypes of e-merchant those with low-margin businesses and those with high-margin businesses. Finally, there are also platforms or marketplaces like Amazon and Etsy.

Problem   What are the different types of error in fraud detection? What determines an e-commerce service's vulnerability? Should e-commerce services optimize for selling or security? Who needs what? In this chapter, we will address these questions.

6.1 Fraud detection errors: Type I and type II

When attempting to detect and prevent payment fraud, e-commerce services may make two types of errors: *false positives* (type I errors), and *false negatives* (type II errors) [128]. In the following table, we describe each error type.

False positives	False positives, also called *type I error*, occur when a payment is suspected of fraud but it is not. A client suspected of fraud could have his payment rejected or delayed in the case the merchant needs to verify the payment.
False negatives	False negatives, also called *type II error*, are errors that occur when a payment fraud remains undetected by the fraud prevention measures and materializes. Chargebacks for fraud reasons are instances of type II errors.

6.2 An e-commerce service's gross margin

To run a sustainable business, merchants need to make a profit. Profit is the amount of funds left after deducting the costs of doing business from a company's revenue.

It is partly described by the *gross margin*, which is calculated from the sell price and the cost of goods sold (COGS) as follows:

$$\begin{aligned}
&\text{Sell price} \\
&- \text{Cost of goods sold (COGS)} \\
&= \textbf{Gross margin}.
\end{aligned} \qquad (6.1)$$

6.3 An e-commerce service's tolerance to payment fraud

After having described the two types of *errors* when preventing payment fraud and the *gross margin* for an e-commerce service, below, we also introduce the concept of *tolerance* to payment fraud.

Tolerance to payment fraud
An e-commerce service's capacity to endure payment frauds

> The *tolerance* of an e-commerce service to payment fraud is its capacity to endure payment fraud without being adversely impacted.

Given this definition of the *tolerance* to payment fraud, we postulate that the lower the *gross margin* of an e-commerce service, the lower its *tolerance* to payment fraud. In the opposite, the higher its *gross margin*, the greater its *tolerance*.

Whether an e-commerce service is *tolerant* or *intolerant* to payment fraud changes what the e-commerce service optimizes.

Tolerant If an e-commerce service is *tolerant*, it strives to sell as much as possible and acquires payments at a *lower security level*.

Intolerant If an e-commerce service is *intolerant* to payment fraud, it needs to avoid payment fraud and therefore it needs to acquire payments at a *high security level*.

6.4 Selling or security: Who needs what

In previous sections we described how e-commerce services optimize security or selling depending on their *tolerance* to payment fraud. Now, we review and give examples for each possibility, i.e., *selling* or *security*.

Selling Those who are more interested in reducing the number of payments thought to be fraudulent when they are not (type I, false positives [128]) are *high margin merchants, issuers* when 3D Secure is enabled, and *acquirers and PSPs* when 3D Secure is disabled.

High margin merchants	The merchants that have a high margin tend to prefer to absorb a few fraud cases, rather than impacting most of their customers.
3DS-disabled Issuers	Issuers have limited incentives to prevent payment fraud when 3D Secure is disabled.
3DS-enabled Acquirers and PSPs	The incentives to prevent payment fraud are limited when 3D Secure is enabled because issuing banks are liable.

Security Those who need to reduce the number of undetected frauds (type II, false negatives [128]) and need *security* are *low margin merchants, marketplaces, issuers* when 3D Secure is enabled, and *acquirers and PSPs* when 3D Secure is disabled.

Low margin merchants	Low margin merchants are exposed to the risk that fraudulent payments materialize as chargebacks. Therefore, they tend to favor security over selling.
Market-places	Marketplaces aim to be stricter when processing payments so that sellers trust the platform and continue to do business there [64].

| 3DS-enabled Issuers | Because issuers are liable in case of fraud when 3D Secure is enabled, issuers favor security over selling. |
| 3DS-disabled Acquirers and PSPs | When 3D Secure is disabled and when the merchant cannot refund the principal, then acquirers and PSPs are exposed to the chargeback risk. |

Hence, when selling prevails over security, the focus is on suspecting fewer payments of being fraudulent (type I, false positives). Conversely, when security prevails over selling, the focus is on having fewer frauds undetected (type II, false negatives) [128].

The following table synthesizes whether *selling* or *security* is preferred depending on the type of company.

Selling or security
Company profile determines the type of error optimized

| Error | Focus on | | # | Type of company |
	First	Second		
Type I: false positives or suspicions	Selling	Security	1	Merchant (high margin)
			2	Issuer (3DS-disabled)
			3	Merchant (3DS-enabled)
Type II: false negatives or undetected frauds	Security	Selling	4	Merchant (small margin)
			5	Marketplace
			6	Issuer (3DS-enabled)
			7	Merchant (3DS-disabled)

6.5 #1 criterion for risk level: The geographical reach

To illustrate how *geographical reach* influences the *risk level*, we first introduce the French Observatory for Payment Card Security (OSCP) from the Banque de France [8]. Then we provide a table that summarizes payment fraud per issuing and acquiring zone with data series from the OSCP. And finally we draw conclusions.

The observatory for payment card security
Fraud statistics on payment cards in France

> The observatory for payment card security (OSCP) is an annual report [8] published by the Banque de France that aggregates fraud statistics for card not present (CNP) and card present (CP) transactions in France, the Single Euro Payments Area (SEPA) zone, and worldwide payment cards acquired in France.

The statistics from the OSCP report indicate that the farther away the payment card is from the acquiring country (France, in this case), the greater the risk.

6.6 #2 criterion for risk level: The catalog of product

A second aspect that influences the risk is the catalog of products and services being traded; in the table below we list instances of product categories that have *high* and *low* fraud rates.

Specific products like spare parts or customized products are hard to resell on the black market because there is little demand for such

Fraud per issuing and acquiring zone
Cross-border payments bear 4x higher risk

Acquirer's origin	Metrics	Issuer's origin		
		France	SEPA	World
France	Fraud volume	0.14B€	0.02B€	0.03B€
	Sales volume	62.51B€	4.67B€	2.77B€
	Fraud rate	0.22%	0.42%	1.08%
	Ratio	1.0x	1.9x	4.9x
SEPA	Fraud volume	0.09B€		
	Sales volume	8.83B€		
	Fraud rate	1.02%		
	Ratio	4.6x		
World	Fraud volume	0.02B€		
	Sales volume	2.06B€		
	Fraud rate	0.97%		
	Ratio	4.4x		

Sources: data series published in 2015 by the Banque de France [8]

Risk by business domain
How resellable products are determines risk level

Risk level	#	Business area
High	1	Airline tickets
	2	High-tech products
	3	Sportswear
	4	Luxury items
Low	5	Spare parts
	6	Customized products

products. Therefore, they tend to have a very limited exposure to payment fraud.

Though, in some cases fraudsters have been extremely creative in exploiting e-commerce services. Next, we expose the case of Red Box Instant, an online video service operated by Verizon that was shut down in October 2014.

Hacking to test credit cards
Because tested cards are more valuable on the blackmarket

> In the case of Red Box Instant, it is likely that hackers registered fake client accounts to associate information from stolen payment cards with those accounts [47, 16] and, in turn, to test the validity of that information for reselling it.
>
> Indeed, such tested information has a premium value on the black market when compared to untested payment cards. This price difference (or arbitrage) was the opportunity.

Therefore, what looked like a business protected against payment fraud (i.e., a business that rented online videos) turned out to be a very attractive target for hackers. Other creative fraud mechanisms exist, notably in the game industry.

6.7 Who is vulnerable: Key points

In brief

When preventing payment fraud, e-commerce services make two types of errors: *type I* errors or *false positives* and *type II* errors or *false negatives*. The former occurs when a payment is suspected of fraud and it is not. The latter occurs when a fraud has remained undetected and materializes as a chargeback.

The tolerance of an e-commerce service determines whether it optimizes *selling* or *security* when processing payments. In general, when selling prevails over security, the focus is on reducing the rate of false positives. And when security prevails over selling, the focus is on reducing the rate of false negatives.

6 Who is vulnerable to payment fraud

Different factors influence the risk level of payment fraud for e-commerce services. Among those, the *geographic reach* and the *catalog of products* are two main criteria.

Key points

- False positives (type I errors) are true clients suspected of fraud.

- False negatives (type II errors) are real frauds that remained undetected.

- If selling prevails over security, the focus is on reducing the rate of false positives.

- If security prevails over selling, the focus is on reducing the rate of false negatives.

- A business's tolerance to payment fraud is its capacity to absorb the costs associated with a payment fraud.

- A business's risk level is the frequency (%) of fraud attempts and confirmed frauds it has experienced.

- A business's gross margin determines its *tolerance* to fraud.

- A business's geographical reach and catalog of products are the two main criteria that determine its risk level.

- Cross-border payments have a risk level four times higher than that of domestic payments in France.

III | Preventing fraud: How to make it work

Background

In the first part, we reviewed several *methods* that enable a giver to transfer the ownership of a product or service by means of a payment to a receiver.

Then, we reviewed the *entities* that make online payments possible, notably with payment cards. The intermediaries include the cardholder; the cardholder's bank (the issuer); the card schemes; the merchant; the merchant's bank; the acquiring service; and, in some cases, the settling bank.

Next, we reviewed the three-step *process* for paying online with payment cards. This process starts with initiating the *conditions* to make online payments possible. It continues with *exchanging the counterparty* and finishes with *fulfilling the order*.

In most cases, things go right when paying online, but in some instances, payments may fail. We reviewed this idea in the second part. We analyzed some reasons why things may go wrong when processing payments, particularly *payment fraud*.

Problem

In this part, we focus on the problem of detecting, managing, and preventing payment fraud when processing payments online. We also look at the array of existing solutions offered by the online payment industry.

Outline

In the first chapter, we describe the *landscape* of fraud prevention solutions. Then we provide a *bird's-eye view* of the payment fraud prevention process. Next, we *dive deep into the bits and pieces* of fraud detection. The last chapter describes the *feedback loop*, i.e., fraud prevention process auditing.

7 | Fraud prevention solutions: The landscape

Background   The existence of arbitrage opportunities, i.e., price differences between markets, creates an inevitable driving force for payment fraud to occur.

One approach to prevent payment fraud is to avoid data leaks, which is the domain of cybersecurity; another is to strengthen the authentication mechanisms of payment methods, which is the domain of payment processing intermediaries. Yet another is to proactively manage payment fraud with fraud detection software.

Problem   In this chapter, we describe the landscape of options to prevent the risk of payment fraud for issuers and online merchants.

7.1 Fraud prevention: For issuers

As part of the landscape of fraud prevention solutions when processing online payments, first we describe the array of methods that *issuing banks* use.

To help reduce fraud, issuers may authenticate card holders with two factors (3D Secure). The first factor is the card number and CVC, and the second is, generally, the phone number or email address linked to the card holder, which is used to receive authentication codes.

Using private banking contracts or client-defined rules, banks can also limit the maximum amount a card is charged within a given period (e.g., a week or a month) or the regions from which charges can come (e.g., national or international). These limits also help reduce the likelihood of fraud.

Another layer of prevention for banks involves algorithms that can identify live transactions at risk for payment fraud. If these algorithms detect a risky transaction, alerts are triggered. These alerts may notify the bank or the client. At that point, there are three options: to *deny*, *verify*, or *accept* transactions.

Payment alerts triggered by issuing banks

Refuse, suggest a verification, or accept by default a payment

#	Outcome	Reason
1	Refuse	A blacklist is hit.
2	Verify	If payment validation mechanisms exist, client or bank verifies the payment.
3	Accept	If client does not respond after alert rapidly, transaction defaults to accepted.

Then, issuers must know exactly what their *liabilities* are for each fraud subtype. Depending on those liabilities, they may shift the loss to the *acquiring side* or the *cardholders*.

Liability shift reasons for issuers

The cardholders and acquiring side also have responsibilities

#	Liability	Reason
1	Acquiring side	3D Secure was disabled.
2	Cardholder	Client failed to rapidly discover the fraudulent charge and notify its bank.

In both cases, because the issuer knows what its liabilities are, it does not "absorb" the losses.

Issuers may also implement internal mechanisms to *speed up the detection and escalation* of fraud. This matters because efficient escalation prevents the repeated occurrence of fraudulent transactions of the same type, which in turn reduces the overall risk and the likelihood that the issuer will have to "absorb" additional losses.

Finally, the issuers' last line of defense is still *insurance*. By definition, issuers have a strong financial incentive to reduce their reliance on insurance because the price of premiums depend on the risk level; the lower that risk, the lower the premium price is.

7.2 Fraud prevention: 3D Secure for merchants

In previous section we described the methods used by *issuers* to reduce their exposure to payment fraud. Henceforth, we shift the focus back to the *merchants*. In particular, here we detail the 3D Secure mechanism, its advantages and inconveniences.

To protect themselves against *illegitimate chargebacks*, e-commerce services have the option to use 3D Secure [49], i.e., a mechanism to authenticate cardholders with two-factors. In the following table, we summarize the 3D Secure versions of Visa, MasterCard, and American Express.

3D Secure brand identities

Card networks have brand identities of 3D Secure

Card brand	Mechanism
Visa	Verified by Visa
MasterCard	MasterCard SecureCode
American Express	AMEX SafeKey

Sources: MasterCard Payment Gateway Services [40]

In practice, a 3D Secure authentication for a buyer is a sequence of four steps, which we summarize in the following table.

By using 3D Secure, e-commerce services know that the cardholders are authenticated with two factors, which reduces the likelihood that the payments made are fraudulent, but merchants are also insured against the losses due to payment fraud. This protection is called the *liability shift*.

If the buyer successfully completes the 3D Secure challenge, then the merchant is granted the guarantee of the payment. However, if the client does not successfully complete the challenge and the merchant still wants to process the payment, then the merchant is

3D Secure sequence of steps

Card details are acquired, then issuer authenticates client

#	At	Factor	Description
1	Merchant	1	Cardholder inputs its credit card number and CVC code.
2	Payment provider	-	Payment provider redirects to issuer's 3D Secure authentication page.
3	Issuer	2	Cardholder answers challenge: password, birthdate, code sent to phone or email.
4	Merchant	-	Cardholder redirected to merchant's website by issuer.

liable when the payment is a fraud.

Liability shift

The *liability shift* is a sort of insurance for payments made with 3D Secure authentication. It protects merchants against the losses due to payment fraud by transferring the responsibility to the issuing banks, whose role was to authenticate the cardholder. However, *limits apply* to the liability shift.

For example, if more than 2% of an e-commerce service's sales volume is fraudulent, the card networks will look carefully at the merchant account and, if the fraud rate does not reduce rapidly, the e-commerce service may become liable for the 2%+ chargebacks.

And if the situation does not improve, the e-commerce service may lose its ability to accept payments from this card brand, which is a catastrophic scenario for a merchant.

Although 3D Secure looks like an ideal solution for merchants, it is not. There are many circumstances when 3D Secure may fail. Seven notable 3D Secure failure reasons are reported below.

3D Secure failure reasons
Cumulatively, these failures reduce the conversion

#	Reasons
1	Authentication system is down.
2	Bank has not yet implemented 3D Secure.
3	Card is not 3D Secure enabled.
4	Challenge sends an SMS but buyer does not have the phone nearby.
5	Code is sent to an incorrect phone number.
6	Phone is turned off.
7	Phone does not have a signal, e.g., in a basement or abroad.

Taken cumulatively, these failures hurt payment conversion and reduce revenue opportunities for merchants. This is why some merchants with a limited payment risk have decided to forego two-factor authentication.

7.3 Fraud prevention: In-house, legacy, and dedicated

We first introduced fraud prevention methods for issuers and the use of 3D Secure for merchants. Now, we examine the landscape of *fraud detection systems* for merchants.

7.3 Fraud prevention: In-house, legacy, and dedicated

We see three types of fraud detection systems: those that a business can develop *in-house*, those from *legacy* payment tech vendors, and those provided by *dedicated vendors*.

In-house systems
These systems are useful when businesses need to get started and react quickly. They just need to know how to program the payment flow.

However, programming the fraud prevention rules in-house does not scale. Expertise will be a limiting factor down the road. Managing rules may become a pain, especially if the person who creates the rules leaves the company.

Legacy systems
These systems come from commercial banks and payment service providers. If the e-commerce service's needs are limited, these systems are conceptually simple and good to start with.

This may be the case if the merchant operates in its country of origin and accepts only domestic cards. However, some payment service providers have customizable fraud detection systems whose performance approaches the one of *dedicated systems*.

Dedicated systems
Dedicated fraud detection systems exist for large retailers who need the safety conferred by large service providers.

There are also a range of start-ups. These are the best choice when innovation, domain-specific expertise, automation, and price competitiveness are necessary.

7.4 Fraud prevention: Which one to choose?

After describing the range of options available to e-commerce services to prevent payment fraud, now we provide guidance on how to choose the best approach.

Notably, it is likely that if the gross margin is low, the *tolerance* to payment fraud is limited and the *risk level* is medium or high. In practice, the history of payment fraud determines the actual *exposure* to payment fraud. Next, we describe the possible options for an e-commerce service if it has a *low*, *medium*, or *high risk*.

Low risk   If the business is low risk (or is just starting out), it might simply do without a fraud prevention system. Alternatively, it could also enable 3D Secure, which would prevent any chargeback to materialize.

Some examples of low risk e-commerce services are those that sell customizable or products that are hard to resell on the black market.

Medium risk   If the business has a medium risk, an in-house solution is generally inadvisable. However, the merchant might consider 3D Secure and/or a legacy or dedicated fraud detection system.

The best choice depends on the overall exposure to payment fraud and the tolerance to the risk. Some examples of medium-risk e-commerce services include most of the retail industry that sells online (e.g., clothing, branded products, entertainment).

High risk   Finally, if the business has a high risk, it should definitely opt for a dedicated fraud detection system, with or without 3D Secure.

Some examples of high-risk e-commerce services are those that sell high-tech products, the game industry, and online travel agents.

7.5 Fraud prevention solutions: Key points

In brief

Issuers prevent payment fraud by implementing several risk-reducing strategies, such as contracts, card usage limits, fraud detection algorithms, blacklists, insurance, and 3D Secure verification.

With 3D Secure, the liability for payment fraud is transferred to the issuers. However, many failure reasons hurt payment conversion and reduce revenue opportunities for merchants.

There are in-house-developed fraud detection systems, systems provided by legacy payment tech providers, and systems provided by companies whose principal business is that of fraud prevention.

If its risk level is low, an e-commerce service may do without a fraud prevention solution or just use 3D Secure. It may opt for 3D Secure and/or a legacy or dedicated fraud prevention system if its risk level is medium. It may use a dedicated system if its risk level is high.

Key points

- Issuers use *multiple layers* of security to protect themselves against payment fraud.

- 3D Secure shifts liability to issuers, thereby protecting merchants.

- 3D Secure failures hurt conversion and revenue opportunities.

- A merchant may manage the risk of payment fraud in-house with legacy systems or with vendors of dedicated solutions.

- The business's tolerance and risk level determine which type of fraud prevention solution it should choose.

- The lower the tolerance and the higher the risk, the more likely it is that a merchant will need a dedicated fraud prevention solution.

8 Fraud prevention process: A bird's-eye view

Background   In previous chapter we reviewed the landscape of fraud prevention solutions. For *issuers*, we described a series of risk reducing security measures and for *merchants* we described 3D Secure and fraud detection systems as two security layers that can be used together or separately to reduce payment fraud risk.

Now, businesses tend to carry out tasks by means of *processes*, whose goal is to streamline the operation of businesses and gain reliability, quality, and cost-effectiveness. Fraud prevention is an additional business process.

Problem   Therefore, we wonder what is the typical task sequence of a fraud prevention process for an e-commerce service?

8.1 Two data types

The first step of the payment fraud prevention process is to *collect data* about how clients register and use the e-commerce service. Essentially two data types exist: *longitudinal* and *cross-sectional*.

Longitudinal   Longitudinal data refers to measurements that vary in time. They are also commonly called time series.

Cross-sectional   Cross-sectional data refers to measurements whose value do not change over time.

It matters to differentiate the two data types because the data collection, data processing, and data storage mechanisms differ significantly between longitudinal and cross-sectional data.

In the table below we list examples of *cross-sectional* and *longitudinal* data attributes.

Longitudinal and cross-sectional

Longitudinal data vary in time; cross-sectional data does not

Data type	Example
Longitudinal	The amount of money spent on the service
	The changes in the user profile
	The user logins
Cross-sectional	The first name and last name
	The date of birth
	The login subscribe date
	The signup device

8.2 Before the payment: Control the signup process

Previously, we described two data types, i.e., *cross-sectional* and *longitudinal* data. Now, we examine how an e-commerce service can *control the signup process* of its clients based on risks.

At first, the enrollment process should be properly tracked with analytics so that if a case of fraud is reported on a transaction, a *post mortem* analysis can reveal fraud markers. Then, discovering these markers may help the e-commerce service take preventive measures, such as those listed in the table below.

Controlled signup process

Control measures may help limit fraud risk

#	Measures
1	Prohibit some product categories.
2	Refuse some types of buyers (and sellers if this is a marketplace).
3	Closely monitor transactions known to bear a high risk.

As an instance of a controlled signup process, we consider Uber's signup process and see how they do in practice.

Uber's signup process
Tracking user's signup; verifying data; and gamification

The signup process requires the user to provide: her account credentials (email, password); her account details (first name, last name, mobile phone number, language); and a payment method (card number, CCV, month, year, zip code).

Also, additional data is logged automatically like: the IP address (and its geolocation); the timestamps; the type of browser (if the signup occurs from a desktop); and the phone characteristics (if the signup occurs from a mobile device).

Notably, Uber relies on geolocation for its service; that information is provided while the app is in the foreground and when it is in the background. Finally, Uber uses a data hub to centralize the data streams and make them accessible to all departments.

To make sure the email address and mobile phone number are correct, Uber also sends emails with a verification link and SMS messages with a code which, meanwhile, allows the service to collect additional information about the client. This matters because possible inconsistencies during the signup process may be early indicators of a risk of payment fraud.

Uber has also gamified the process of completing a user's profile. In particular, there is a percent-complete score and a series of questions with shaded checkmarks that prompt the user to complete her profile. Again, these steps are additional layers of security for the service: the more complete the profile, the lower the risk.

Last, the user may link her other accounts (e.g., Spotify and Pandora), which helps know how old the other social accounts are and how many connections there are on each account. What matters here is not the individual but the cumulative risk-reducing effects of the data collection, verification, and linking mechanisms.

8.3 Before the payment: Engineer trust

Ideally, an absence of payment fraud is attainable if there is a *complete trust* between the buyers and the seller, but because 100 percent trust is unachievable, some marketplaces *engineer trust*, thereby reducing risk for buyers and sellers.

Below, we describe four aspects when engineering trust: the use of *reviews*, the fact that *credibility builds over time*, the technique of *transferring credibility from socials*, and the use of *bios and verified phones*.

Reviews Airbnb, for example, lets request or provide reviews, which helps buyers and sellers build credibility and, in turn, trust. Others, like eBay and Amazon display the number of transactions and/or the average ratings of profiles.

These are extremely useful when evaluating the level of risk because it is unlikely that sellers and buyers with a good record of sales are scammers.

Credibility builds over time

However, credibility metrics are built over time, which makes it harder for real buyers or sellers who are starting out and thus have no credibility yet, to make sales quickly and effectively, because they are viewed as presenting a higher risk.

Transfer credibility from socials

One way Airbnb and, to a lesser extent, eBay and Amazon, address this is to allow buyers and sellers to build their own credibility by linking their buyer or seller profiles to other social profiles, e.g., Facebook, Twitter, or Google+. This way, the credibility established on other social networks is transferred to the e-commerce service.

Bios and verified phones

In addition, Airbnb provides bios, adds phone numbers that have been authenticated with short codes, and verifies emails with activation links.

Combined, these mechanisms greatly help reduce the level of risk of the transaction as perceived by buyers and sellers before the sale and, as observed after it is completed.

To conclude this section on *credibility building* and the *engineering of trust*, we review how a near real time e-commerce service like Uber may manage its risk.

Credibility building exemplified on Uber
A short time to first use of the service means a higher risk level

On the other hand, if the calculated risk is significant, the service may limit how much the user can use the service, e.g., spending less than $20 in a new city or country where the service has just been rolled out. Later, as trust in the user increases or if the transaction history shows that payments are safe in this context, limits may be lifted.

Though, with services that compete with one another (e.g., Uber and Lyft), it is important to limit friction during user on-boarding and during customers' regular use of the service. Hence, companies must carefully weigh the benefits of protection against the losses in revenue opportunities when implementing limits to protect against payment fraud. Companies can estimate this tradeoff every month, every day, or for each transaction.

On the other hand, if the calculated risk is significant, the service may limit how much the user can use the service, e.g., spending less than $20 in a new city or country where the service has just been rolled out. Later, as trust in the user increases or if the transaction history shows that payments are safe in this context, limits may be lifted.

Though, with services that compete with one another (e.g., Uber and Lyft), it is important to limit friction during user on-boarding and during customers' regular use of the service. Hence, companies must carefully weigh the benefits of protection against the losses in revenue opportunities when implementing limits to protect against payment fraud. Companies can estimate this tradeoff every month, every day, or for each transaction.

8.4 After the payment: Score the risk

If analytics tend to describe what's happening, which is already a big step forward, the game-changing approach implements statistical models that can predict the level of the risk dynamically before, during, and, in some cases, after transactions.

These algorithms classify or score events based on a series of markers that describe their characteristics. Then, based on the results of these algorithms, i.e., a class like accept or reject or a score like a likelihood of fraud (%), a specific treatment may be defined that says how to "handle" the fraud suspicious cases.

Typically, there are three ways to handle outcomes fraud suspicious cases, i.e., to *accept, verify,* or *reject* a transaction.

Outcomes of detection algorithms
Three options: to accept, verify, or reject transactions

#	Outcome	Transaction
1	Accept	Automatically accepted, e.g., if it hits a whitelist.
2	Verify	Sent for manual verification by an analyst.
3	Reject	Automatically rejected, e.g., if it hits a blacklist.

With predictive analytics, there are an infinite number of possibilities for refining how risk is detected, prevented, and handled. If it is appropriately used, predictive analytics may help boost trust on the e-commerce service and, in turn, increase revenue.

8.5 After the risk score: Verify payments manually

Due to its limited reviewing capacity, an e-commerce service needs to prioritize payments that carry the highest risk while automatically accepting the rest. To identify the payments with the highest risk, filtering mechanisms exist. Notably, rules and machine learning-based selectors exist.

The typical review rate for an e-commerce service ranges between 1 and 10% of the payments. If the tolerance of the merchant for payment fraud is low, the review rate tends to be higher.

However, the review rate between an issuer and a merchant differs significantly. It is highly unlikely that an issuer can even think of manually reviewing 1% of the payments from its cardholders; more likely, it verifies 0.1% to 0.01%.

Because manual reviewers won't always know whether to accept a payment on their own, the e-commerce service may reach out to the customer for further verification. The way in which it makes the verification depends, notably, on the following:

- the merchant's and the client's locations;

- the forms of ID requested; and

- the type of e-commerce service.

Parts of this payment verification process are very simple, such as managing CRM. E-commerce services can figure them out themselves. Others are very advanced, so they demand expertise, particularly in digital forensics; having access to expert reviewers may be needed.

8.6 After order fulfillment: Manage chargebacks

On average, issuing banks only notify merchants of fraud cases four weeks after the payment date, but this can take as long as six months; the figure below illustrates the typical escalation time.

Hence, a lot of time passes between when the products are shipped and when the money is withdrawn from the merchant's bank account due to a chargeback. It can get even worse if additional fraud has occurred and the merchant did not spot it in time.

To react to fraud cases and failed fraud attempts, the typical next step is to find the common denominator. Then, merchants make some rules to prevent additional fraud of that type.

However, because merchants are *reactive*, this means that fraudsters tend to have an edge over merchants because merchants are always too late unless they fundamentally change the way in which fraud is prevented, which is the challenge that some startups are addressing.

Time needed to escalate a chargeback
30 days in average; up to six months

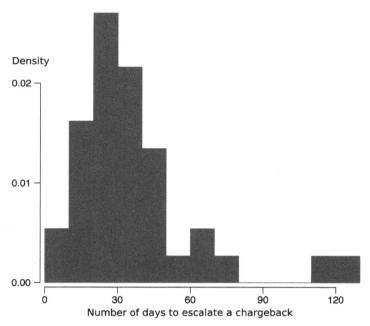

Sources: Ubivar.com client

8.7 Fraud prevention process: Key points

In brief

Uber uses a *data hub* service to gather its users' data usage analytics, centralize them, and make them available to all departments.

In marketplaces like Airbnb, eBay, and Amazon, helping users build their credibility can, in turn, reduce the risk of payment fraud; this is the concept of engineering trust.

Statistical models predicting the payment's risk level may classify payments as low, medium, and high risk, thereby directing orders for *automatic acceptance, manual verification,* or *direct rejection.*

Risk operation analysts may reach out to the clients for additional proofs of identity. Depending on the business, from 0.1% to 10% of the payments are reviewed by risk operation analysts.

Several weeks are necessary to escalate chargebacks to merchants. Merchants may accept chargebacks and refund cardholders or defend the cases if they are not liable for the losses.

Key points

- Preventing payment fraud includes collecting data, scoring the risk, manually verifying payments, and managing chargebacks.

- Tracking clients during their onboarding and shopping is important; companies like Uber use a *data hub* service.

- Marketplaces reduce their overall risk by *engineering trust.*

- Scoring algorithms help prioritize high-risk payments.

- Risk operation analysts verify high-risk payments.

- The *escalation time* is the time between the payment and the chargeback notification to the merchant.

- Chargebacks are often analyzed retrospectively to discover what went wrong through post-mortem analyses.

- Merchants *react* to payment frauds, which means fraudsters tend to have an edge over merchants.

9   Deep dive into fraud detection: Bits and pieces

Background   In previous chapter, we provided a bird's-eye view of what a complete fraud prevention process looks like. In practice, each component of the fraud prevention process has a specialized set of tools and methods, which we call the *bits and pieces*.

Problem   What are the different components of a fraud prevention process? What are the configuration possibilities of each component? What are the pros and cons of each component? These are the questions we will address in this chapter.

9.1 Multi-factor authentication: Back to 3D Secure

Multi-factor authentication aims to grant access to computer systems (e.g., Internet banking) using several pieces of evidence from the user, such as a knowledge factor, a possession factor, or an inherence factor.

Knowledge factor	Login and password	These are the most common form of authentication. For PayPal, only a login name and password are necessary to make payments.
Possession factor	Payment card	Possession factors are the payment cards on which digits are printed on the front of the cards and CVC codes are written on the back. However, payment cards are becoming another knowledge factor because cardholders store their cards online.
	Mobile phone	They are frequently used as possession factors, notably for 3D Secure where SMSs with passcodes are sent to cardholders.
	Mobile apps	Applications also exist to generate security codes with momentary validity.

	Driven by open time-based one-time password algorithms; these are similar to the security tokens described above.
Security tokens	Online banking often uses security tokens, small devices that help users prove their identities electronically, e.g., by storing cryptographic keys or passwords or by using small keypads and screens to authenticate users.
USB sticks	USB sticks also exist with embedded RFID chips. With the press of a button, a cryptographic string is sent back to authenticate the user; Yubico is one of manufacturer of such devices.
Inherence factor	Biometrics	Associated with the user, these include face recognition, fingerprint identification, retina scan, iris scan, and signature or voice analysis.

Each authentication mechanism has its *pros and cons*, which make it suitable or unsuitable when authenticating online payments. Below, we examine 3D Secure and facial recognition.

3D Secure In response to the drops in conversion due to 3D Secure, it is possible that issuers will shift away from possession factors (which may be too burdensome) to knowledge factors. The return in conversion will likely offset the marginal cost of the increased risk.

Facial recognition *Biometric authentication* is regulated, notably in France where a declaration by the National Council for Data Privacy is required.

Given the existing authentication methods, biometrics authentication mechanism vendors may have to demonstrate how their technology significantly improves the performance of fraud prevention.

Moreover, while AI algorithms are capable of recognizing road conditions (e.g., for Tesla's self-driving cars) or faces (e.g., for photo software), facial recognition algorithms may still have issues differentiating real people from photos (or forged faces) over the range of real-life lighting and contrast conditions.

This means facial recognition remains subject to *counterfeit* which is what it should address in the first place. Hence, facial recognition may not be cost effective yet compared to more traditional authentication.

9.2 List-based mechanisms: White-, gray-, and blacklists

Whitelists; *graylists*, which are also called custom lists; and *black-lists*, which are also called block lists, offer basic access control mechanisms to *allow*, *limit*, or *prevent* a group of clients to buy products or services from an e-commerce vendor.

The principle of lists is straightforward. Order characteristics, such as the email, the IP address, or the phone number are added to lists, and if a client who makes a purchase is on one of these lists, his or her order is allowed, delayed, or stopped as appropriate.

Below we describe with more details the three types of lists, i.e., *whitelists*, *graylists*, and *blacklists*.

Lists White — These lists are designed to identify clients who are exempt from payment fraud.

This is notably the case for clients from marketplaces like Amazon, which perform payment verifications. As well, clients paying with online banking or bank transfers are usually exempt from payment fraud.

Therefore, properly designing whitelists is crucial to prevent running fraud verifications on real clients and diverting scarce merchant resources.

Gray   These lists are used to identify subgroups of clients who share common characteristics, such as email domains, IP countries, or invoice countries.

Client credit cards, emails, IP addresses, or phone numbers added to a list are labelled as such, and points are sometimes added to a sum score, with a certain value indicating the risk level.

Black   Blacklists are often used to prevent credit cards, emails, IP addresses, or phone numbers that were previously used to make fraudulent purchases from being used to make additional purchases.

Alternatively, merchants may rely on blacklists to prevent the use of their e-commerce service by certain types of buyers, e.g., preventing buyers from abroad from using an e-commerce service that operates only in its own country of origin.

In terms of *pros and cons*, white-, gray-, and blacklists have the advantage to be very *simple* to setup, configure, and understand. However, lists will stall or *drift in time* and the lists will lead to more errors of type I or false positives over time. This is a major drawback.

9.3 Rule-based mechanisms: Matching or threshold

The concept of rules is similar to that of whitelists, blacklists and graylists. However, instead of relying on list matches, a rule performs a test, the result of which is usually binary.

There are at least two rule subtypes: *matching* and *threshold* rules.

Types of fraud prevention rules
Rules are either matching or based on a threshold

#	Type	Description
1	Matching	Partial, complete, or regular expression match.
2	Threshold	Less than or greater than a threshold.

Examples of such rules include the following:

- Is this payment made from the United States?

- Is this an order for a high risk product from our catalogue?

- Is this amount greater than the threshold value?

Then, rules have two possible outcomes. They are either *forcing* or *scoring*, which is what the following table summarizes.

Outcomes for fraud prevention
A triggered rule forces a review or add point to the risk score

#	Outcome	Description
1	Forcing	Forces a review by risk operation analysts.
2	Scoring	Add points to a risk score.

In terms of *pros and cons*, rules are also *simple* to setup, configure, and understand, which makes them very attractive initially.

However, rules are difficult to manage over time too, particularly if there are many of them.

Moreover, because rules are expensive to audit and review, the set of rules of the fraud detection system becomes less accurate over time. More false positive or type I errors are made over time, which is another instance of the *drift in time*. This is a major drawback, too.

9.4 Risk scores: Sum score or statistical models

When speaking of risk score to people outside of risk management, the underlying concept is not always clear. In the following we explain the concept of risk score as well as its use.

The concept of scoring
Scoring improves the objectivity when making decisions

> A score is usually a percent number (%) called the likelihood, which refers to the probability that an event will occur.

> Whereas a personal opinion about a risk is subjective, a score is objective because it is data driven.

Hence, institutions use scoring to predict the risk before it occurs, which may help the institution avoid the risk or manage it proactively. To further illustrate the concept of scores, in the following paragraphs we describe how scores apply in *lending*, *insurance*, and *online payment*.

Lending   With lending, scores evaluate the risk that a client will not be able to reimburse the borrowed money; if the score is high, the bank might seek collateral.

Insurance   With insurance, scores predict the risk that a subscriber will be exposed to an accidental loss or a catastrophe event.

Online payment   With payment the event measured is fraud, and the score is the likelihood that the payment will lead to an (illegitimate) reversal.

There are two broad types of risk scores: the *sum scores* and the scores estimated by *statistical models*.

Sum scores   These risk scores are the sum of the individual weights given to the scoring rules hit by the transaction.

The sum score adds points to a total. If the total of the *sum score* is higher than a threshold, the order is sent for verification; the treatment in case of a high score is similar to forcing rules.

Statistical models   These risk scores are statistical models optimized numerically.

> The outcome of statistical models to predict risk is either a number between 0 (0%) and 1 (100%), which reflects the likelihood that a payment is a fraud or a class, e.g., fraud/not-fraud.

In terms of *pros and cons*, sum scores are simple to apprehend and inexpensive to set up. Frequently, this is the first way to build a risk score. However, that simplicity leads to a poor *calibration*, which we define hereafter.

Calibration
How accurately does the model measure fraud/not fraud

Calibration comes from measurement technology. It is the process of comparing a measurement made by a device with a standard, e.g., voltage, meters, or fraud/not fraud.

A difference between the standard and the measurement indicates that the device has a *calibration error*. It does not measure the standard correctly. It is biased. In practice, all devices are biased, and the challenge is to minimize that bias.

Hence, because the weights of the *sum scores* are set manually, they are poorly calibrated with payment fraud. On the other hand, estimating the weights of the *statistical model* with optimization algorithms can lead to risk scores whose calibrations improve dramatically compared to that of a sum score.

However, the better calibration of *statistical models* comes at the expense of complexity and expertise because statistical models are much harder to understand, set up, and manage, especially if they are non-linear. Still, the boost in performance has the potential to greatly offset the cost, and for linear statistical models, people with expertise in statistics will know how to interpret them.

In the following table we summarize the *pros and cons* of *sum scores* and *statistical models* to predict fraud risk.

Sum scores vs statistical models
Despite their added complexity, statistical models are better

Type	Pros	Cons
Sum scores	Simple Inexpensive Easy setup	Poor calibration
Statistical models	Optimal calibration	More expertise needed More complex to manage

9.5 Payment verifications

Manual verification is the process of having reviewers manually check the characteristics of the order being made. Timewise, reviews are either carried out *before shipping* the product or *after the product* is shipped and delivered.

Timing of payment reviews
Reviews are carried out before or after shipping

Time	#	Reason
Before shipping	1	To prevent payment fraud.
After shipping	2	Chargeback has escalated.

Notably, the reviews that are carried out after shipping could be referred as *post mortem* reviews.

Post mortem reviews
To see what went wrong, and what could be improved

> Post mortem reviews exist to figure out what went wrong in the payment verification process and to see what could be improved so this type of chargeback does not repeat.

Now, given the two types of timewise reviews, we also distinguish between three review subtypes, i.e., *normal reviews*, *peer reviews*, and *external peer reviews*.

Three types of payment verifications
Risk operation analysts review payments alone or with peers

Review type	#	Description
Normal review	1	When risk operation analysts evaluate the level of risk of a payment on their own.
Peer-review	2	When analysts request that their colleagues perform a *formal* or an *informal* peer review.
External peer-review	3	When an expert analyst who is not a member of the team is called in to review a payment.

Next, risk operation analysts use several instruments when conducting payment verifications, such as performing *lookups*, consulting *risk statistics*, and *e-mailing* or *telephoning* clients.

Lookup Based on the characteristics of the payment, e.g., the IP address, the email address, the delivery address, etc., reviewers may retrieve all the transactions matching these characteristics.

If that information is not in their IT system, they can also connect to the system from their payment service provider or acquiring service.

In addition, lookups on social media networks, public databases, and mapping websites are also commonly performed.

With look up, risk operation analysts can verify the buying and payment fraud history for each payment characteristics. In turn, a characteristic's track record may help the analyst make an objective decision.

Consult risk statistics Internally, risk operation analysts may have access to histories of payment fraud and to risk statistics.

By extracting such statistics from the database, analysts may improve the objectivity of their manual verifications.

Email client Emails are an additional instrument for risk operation analysts when conducting payment verifications. They use emails to reach out to clients when there are doubts about payments.

Reviewers usually ask the client for a digital copy of official proof of address, e.g., a utility bill, phone contract, or rental contract.

However, one issue with these types of documents is that they can be *counterfeited*. Hence, without proper training in online forensics, the reviewer may not identify forged documents, and the fraud may remain unnoticed.

Phone client   Finally, the reviewer may call the client. Usually, this is a last-resort option because clients do not like calls made to verify payments, especially if:

- the purchase is private and the call is made during office hours; or
- the questions asked lead the client to believe that he or she is suspected of fraud.

In turn, those calls will affect the client's satisfaction and, potentially, his or her lifetime value.

In terms of *pros and cons*, the advantage of payment verifications carried out by risk operation analysts is that they are inexpensive to set up since a CRM, a phone, and an email client are sufficient to get started.

However, payment verifications have several *obvious disadvantages* such as:

- the poor scalability in terms of languages and time shifts;

- the negative impact on client's satisfaction;

- the additional delays, while the payment is queued and waiting to be reviewed; and

- the added risk caused by the additional delays and manual data entries, which may have errors.

Less obviously, the decisions made by reviewers lack calibration, e.g., they may not distinguish between percent differences such as 0.4% and 1.2%, but 1.2% is three times more than 0.4%.

On the other hand, one of the advantages of reviewers is that they are able to make *analogies* by pooling knowledge from diverse sources, thereby relating distant concepts with the case they are reviewing.

9.6 Fraud prevention bits and pieces: Key points

In brief

For 3D Secure, a mobile phone is commonly used as a *possession* factor to receive an SMS. However, to boost conversion during payment, which is one of the major issues with 3D Secure, some issuers may simply use the birth date, i.e., a second *knowledge factor*.

A *whitelisted* client does not undergo fraud screening. *Graylists* may add points to a risk score or force a review. *Blacklists* are used to prevent information that was previously involved in a fraud case from being reused.

Matching and *threshold*-based rules test whether there is a match between the order details and the rule or whether those details are below or above the threshold. They add points to a risk score or force a review.

Risk scores are either *sum scores* whose weights are set manually or *statistical models* whose weights are optimized by algorithms. The latter risk scores outperform the sum scores because the sum scores are poorly calibrated.

Finally, risk operation analysts may carry out simple reviews, peer reviews, and external peer reviews before or after shipping. They run lookups using their IT systems, verify social media networks, consult external databases, and email or phone clients to request proofs of address and verify their identities.

Key points

- *Knowledge, possession,* and *inherence* factors are three types of authentication.

- 3D Secure frequently uses a knowledge and a possession factor, but some issuers also use two knowledge factors.

- Blacklists, graylists, and whitelists help block, limit, or make VIPs the clients.

- *Matching* and *threshold rules* help filter clients based on their details.

- Graylists and rules can be either *scoring* or *forcing rules*.

- Numerically optimized risk scores outperform sum scores, because manually setting their weights lead to a *poor calibration*.

- Payment verifications are carried before and/or after shipping.

- Risk operation analysts carry out reviews independently or with peers inside or outside the company.

- Instruments to verify payments are lookups, risk statistics, social networks, and client contacts.

10 Auditing fraud prevention: The feedback loop

Background In previous chapters, we described the landscape of solutions to prevent payment fraud, provided a bird's-eye view of a typical business process to prevent payment fraud, and dived into the bits and pieces of a fraud prevention system.

Problem One challenge remains. How to evaluate the overall performance of the system as well as the performance of its individual components? This is the problem of designing a feedback loop, auditing the fraud prevention process, and selecting key performance indicators (KPIs).

10.1 The objectives of KPIs

Users of e-commerce services are buyers or sellers and the goal is to facilitate transactions between them with *trust* and *reliability*. However, a series of events may make those transactions unsuccessful. This is what we illustrate in the following table.

Failure reasons of online orders
Orders fail due to issues with payment or fulfillment

#	Reasons
1	Items do not arrive.
2	Items do not match the description.
3	Items are damaged.
4	Payment processing failed.
5	A payment is a fraud.

Therefore, it is crucial to monitor KPIs that provide an accurate snapshot of how well the e-commerce service fulfills the transactions because failed transactions make users of e-commerce services unhappy. If failures repeat, they will lose trust, which will affect the performance of the business.

10.2 The challenge with measuring user fulfillment

How fulfilled the e-commerce service's users are can be measured with a simple binary indicator (e.g., ok or not ok) or with a rating (e.g., 0 to 5 stars). Ratings are the most elementary mechanism to *engineer trust*. In particular, ratings help buyers and sellers build credibility and establish trust in the e-commerce service.

However, each additional user input is known to reduce the transaction *velocity* (cf. "One Click Checkout" from Amazon or "Stay Logged In" from PayPal), which also reduces customer lifetime value and, in turn, the profitability of e-commerce services. Hence, other metrics to measure the performance of the e-commerce service should be used.

10.3 The selection of KPIs

The selection of KPIs depends notably on the *business strategy*, *legal requirements*, and *turnover*.

Business strategy	For some e-commerce businesses, one side (the buyer or the seller) is strategic, which means that transaction success for those users is monitored more precisely than for the other less-strategic user.
Legal obligations	These requirements influence how litigations are arbitrated and how each side is protected. Hence, it is essential to integrate legal requirements when defining KPIs.
Turnover	Turnover determines the resources of the e-commerce service and, therefore, the perimeter of the set of KPIs.

Then, we can classify KPIs into four time groups, i.e., the KPIs that measure performance: *before* the payment; *during* the payment; *after the payment but before* the shipment; and *after the shipment*.

Four time-groups for KPIs
Before, during, and after payment; before or after shipment

#	Time group of KPIs
1	Before the payment.
2	During the payment.
3	After the payment but before the shipment.
4	After the shipment.

Finally, there are the KPIs that measure:

1. how the business performs;

2. how the payment performs;

3. the level of payment fraud; and

4. how the fraud prevention performs.

We cover the *business, payment, payment fraud,* and *fraud prevention* KPIs in the rest of this chapter.

10.4 KPIs for business

Since conversion is king in e-commerce, the #1 and #2 business KPIs are certainly conversion (%) and sales. Along these two KPIs, another important metric is the speed at which payments get fulfilled.

KPIs for business

To measure the performance of the sales pipeline

#	KPI	Description
1	Sales	The total number and volume of sales.
2	Conversion	Proportion of successful transactions.
3	Payment velocity	The speed at which transactions get fulfilled.
	Others	Number of transactions; average cart; minimum cart amount; maximum cart amount.

Then, if the e-commerce services are large enough, those business KPIs can be stratified according to various levels.

KPIs strata to reveal disparities

Risk varies between payment method, region, time period...

#	Strata	Examples
1	Payment method	Visa, Paypal.
2	Geographical area	Country, region.
3	Time period	Hour, day, quarter.
4	Acquisition channel	Socials, search.

10.5 KPIs for payment

It is essential to identify the payments that fail; to search for the root cause of failures; to see if those causes are sporadic; and, if they are not, to attempt prevent their reoccurrence.

Usually, when a charge on a credit card fails, the payment service provider returns a failure code that provides some information. Ideally, each failure code is tracked by its own KPI so that *a posteriori* analyses can reveal the roots of the payment failures.

It's also possible to create compound KPIs that aggregate individual KPIs per failure code into a single, meta-KPI. One way to do so would be to sum up all the payment failure reasons into a single payment failure KPI.

Several instances of payment failure reasons are reported in the following table.

KPIs for payment

To measure payment failure reasons

#	Reasons
1	The customer cancelled the transaction.
2	3D Secure failed.
3	The 3D Secure server was down.
4	The card is not 3D Secure enabled.
5	The funds are insufficient.
6	The card is blacklisted.

10.6 KPIs for fraud

Payment fraud impacts the bottom line of e-commerce services. It is therefore essential to also measure historical fraud trends. There are essentially two fraud subtypes: the frauds where the principal is lost and the frauds where the principal is not lost.

KPIs for fraud

To measure whether the principal is lost or not

#	Principal	Description
1	Not lost	Principal not lost, e.g., because of the liability shift or because the e-commerce service won the defense of the case.
2	Lost	Principal is refunded; this are the "chargebacks."

It is necessary to track the two fraud subtypes, because the financial impact differs between each. Moreover, fraud rates vary significantly between payment methods, with the geographical origin of payments, and with the product type, which means additional KPIs per fraud subtype may be needed.

Finally, these two fraud rates (as well as the volume of transaction and the volume of frauds) are essential to determine if the e-commerce service falls under the *liability shift*, the insurance-like mechanism that protects merchants from chargebacks in case of fraud, when the payment was acquired with 3D Secure.

10.7 KPIs for fraud prevention

If the e-commerce service is exposed to payment fraud, it likely has a fraud prevention system with some rules and scoring in place. In that case, the KPIs are straightforward.

First, the merchant needs to know how many payments the fraud prevention system:

1. accepts automatically;

2. sends for manual verification (if any); and

3. rejects.

Second, because the fraud prevention process makes errors, the e-commerce service needs to know how many instances of fraud were considered ok by:

1. the rules,

2. the risk score, and

3. the risk operation analysts.

These errors are called *false negatives* (or type II); they need to be *minimized*.

Third, with A/B testing, e-commerce services may estimate how many true transactions the rules, scores, and reviewers are rejecting. These are false positives errors (or type I).

KPIs for fraud prevention
To measure the fraud detection outcomes and errors

#	KPI	Proportion of payments
1	Auto-accept	Automatically accepted by the fraud system.
2	Manual review	Sent for manual verification.
3	Reject	Automatically rejected by the fraud system.
4	False positives	True clients suspected of fraud.
5	False negatives	True frauds that the detection has failed to detect.

10.8 Total cost of preventing payment fraud

If possible, the total cost of preventing payment fraud should be estimated. The total cost can integrate some of the following components.

Total cost of preventing payment fraud
It is composed of nine cost elements

Cost of the fraud prevention software	(10.1)
+ Cost of integrating the fraud software (one-off)	(10.2)
+ Cost of maintaining the fraud software	(10.3)
+ Cost of parameterizing that software	(10.4)
+ Cost of the risk operation team	(10.5)
+ Cost of auditing	(10.6)
+ Cost of false positives and false negatives	(10.7)
+ Cost of delivery delays (cf. settlement risk)	(10.8)
+ Cost of lower CLV in case of false positives	(10.9)
= **Total cost of preventing payment fraud**	(10.10)

10.9 Auditing fraud prevention: Key points

In brief

In this chapter, we described how some KPIs reflect how the business stands generally (e.g., turnover, number of transactions, conversion rates, types of payment methods, or geographical distribution of clients).

We also discussed how other KPIs describe how well the risk of payment fraud is managed (e.g., fraud rate and chargeback rate, automatically accepted and rejected transactions, review rate, time per review, rate of cases won and lost) and how well requests from sellers and buyers are handled (e.g., number, response time).

Key points

- Failed payments make clients of e-commerce services *unhappy*.

- Measuring user fulfillment cannot simply rely on surveys because surveys slow down checkout velocity.

- KPIs are defined in function of *business strategy*, *legal* obligations, and *turnover*.

- KPIs are classified in four time groups: before payment, during payment, after payment but before shipment, and after shipment.

- The top business KPIs are sales volume, conversion, and payment velocity.

- The top payment KPIs are those tracking payment failure reasons.

- The top fraud KPIs keep count of fraud cases in which the principal was lost (chargebacks) and those in which it was not.

- The top fraud prevention KPIs are the proportion of auto-accept, manual reviews, auto-reject, false positives, and false negatives.

- The total fraud cost can be estimated; we have outlined nine separate cost factors.

IV   Big data and statistical learning to prevent fraud

Background

In the first part, we reviewed some of the payment methods used to pay online. Then we discussed the different entities involved in carrying out a payment online, which is what we called *passing the witness*. Finally, we described the three steps required to process an online payment.

In the second part, we looked at why things can go wrong when processing online payments and discussed how things go wrong, particularly the processes used to commit payment fraud. Finally, we identified the factors that influence payment fraud.

In the third part, we described the *landscape* of fraud prevention solutions and provided a *bird's-eye view* of the payment fraud prevention process. Then we dived deep into the *bits and pieces* of fraud detection and described the fraud prevention auditing process, which we call the *feedback loop*.

Problem

In this part, we focus on the application of big data, artificial intelligence (AI), and machine learning (ML) to boost the prevention, detection, and management of payment fraud.

Outline

First, we review the preliminary conditions to carry out data analyses for fraud prevention. Second, we describe the essential methods used to measure risk and test hypotheses. Finally, we discuss how it is possible to teach machines to predict a concept like payment fraud.

11 | Preliminary considerations for data analysis

Background Data analyses to prevent the risk of payment fraud in e-commerce services involves collecting data about clients' buying processes, cleaning the data, transforming the data, and modeling payment fraud to support decision-making.

Problem However, to carry out data analyses, a set of scientific methods are used to make measurements and design experiments. It's important to review them, share their definition, and describe their applications. Moreover, as we focus on payment fraud, what is its precise definition?

11.1 Variables and their different subtypes

In Latin, the word variābilis means variable. It is composed of two words: vari(us) and -ābilis, which mean various and -able, i.e., capable of changing [130].

Hence, a variable is what mathematicians, computer scientists, and researchers use to keep track of changes in values, e.g., over time, of a quality [63] or quantity [72] of interest.

Qualitative variable   A quality of interest could be the bestselling color for t-shirts sold per week, and the values overtime could be dark blue, dark blue, yellow, and blue for each of the last four weeks. A quality could also be the fraud risk for a specific month, e.g., low or medium, and the values for the last four months could be low, low, low, and medium.

While the bestselling color for t-shirts is unordered, the fraud risk is. Its three possible values could be low, medium, and high. Hence, qualitative variables with no intrinsic ordering are called *nominal*, whereas ordered qualitative variables are called *ordinal* [17].

Quantitative variable   A quantity of interest could be the revenue generated by the e-commerce service on the last weekend, e.g., $20,000, and its values over the last four weekends could be $12,000, $15,000, $18,000, and $20,000.

A quantity could also be the time of the day for peak sales, e.g., 9:00–12:00, and this peak traffic may have varied over the last four days: 9:00–12:00, 9:00–12:00, 12:00–15:00, and 9:00–12:00.

While the time of day for peak traffic for the e-commerce service is a quantitative variable of type *interval,* the last hour's number of sales is a *ratio* [17].

From the viewpoint of statistics, it is important to identify the variable type because the statistical methods are different [17]. For quantitative variables, *parametric statistics* that rely on the estimation of averages and standard deviations (parameters) are used, but estimating averages for qualitative variables does not make sense. Hence, for qualitative variables, so-called *non-parametric statistics* are used, e.g., counting or categorizing.

In the table below we summarize the different subtypes of quantitative and qualitative variables, indicate the range of applicable statistics, and give examples for each variable subtype.

11.2 Experiments and their design

Previously, we described *quantitative* and *qualitative* variables and the range of statistical methods that apply to each variable type. In this section we introduce the concept of an *experimental design.*

In Latin, the word *experiment* comes from experīmentum, which itself comes from experientia, i.e., an experience or a trial. An experiment is a test under controlled conditions made to either

Applicable statistics per variable type
Two sets of statistical methods for two types of variables

		Non-parametric statistics	Parametric statistics	Examples
Quali-tative	**Nominal**	counts, categories, χ^2, ...		color, fraud status
	Ordinal			level of risk (low, high)
Quanti-tative	**Interval**		averages, variance, bell curve, ...	9:00–12:00 o'clock
	Ratio			\$12,000 or 2%

demonstrate a known truth, examine the validity of a hypothesis, or determine the efficacy of something previously untried [2].

Two types of experiments exist: *experimental* and *non-experimental* studies.

Experimental A study is experimental or interventional when control is deliberately exercised over the treatment.

The treatment could be whether payments are tested against automated fraud prevention mechanisms to evaluate whether these mechanisms reduce risk.

Experimental studies are often called A/B tests [50], trials [2], or knockouts [90].

Non-Experimental In contrast, non-experimental (or observational) studies let nature take its course [2]; no control is exercised over the treatment.

Two subtypes of *non-experimental* studies exist: *descriptive* studies and *analytic* studies [2].

Descriptive *Descriptive* (or exploratory) studies do not try to explain a theory; for example, they just describe frequencies of the phenomenon (payment fraud).

Examples of descriptive studies are the Nilson Report [38], which publishes news and statistics about the card and mobile payment industry and the Observatory for Payment Card Security (OSCP) of the Banque de France [8].

Analytic In contrast, *analytic* studies attempt to test hypotheses and provide explanations about the phenomenon.

Examples of analytic studies are those in which relationships between the exposure, e.g., fraud, and the outcomes, e.g., the payment method, such as Visa, MasterCard, and PayPal, are searched for.

Examples of *non-experimental* (or observational) study designs are *cohort studies*, *case-control studies*, and *surveys*.

Cohort   *Cohort* studies [2], which are also known as *longitudinal* or *prospective*, focus on the development of a phenomenon like payment fraud.

Cohort members may be cardholders. They are studied over an extended period. Some members will be "exposed," e.g., by being victims of identity theft, which is what the analysis aims to reveal.

On the other hand, a cohort can also measure an exposure to a positive outcome like that of repeat-purchases. The aim could be to measure the Client's Lifetime Value (CLV), i.e., the total value of its repeat purchases over a period of time [75].

Case-control   *Case-control* studies [2] compare two groups: a group of cases that has been exposed to payment fraud, for example, and a group of controls that has not been exposed.

These studies are common in machine learning (ML) and artificial intelligence (AI).

Surveys   Finally, *surveys* [2] assess whether the members of a group have been exposed to the phenomenon, e.g., payment fraud.

Alternatively, the survey could also aim to measure the intention to recommend a service to someone else, which is referred to as the Net Promoter Score (NPS) [107].

In contrast to longitudinal studies, these studies are called cross-sectional because they are done at one point in time.

The following table summarizes the different types of research methods and their possible use in the context of e-commerce services.

Research methods
Case-control for ML and AI; randomization for A/B testing

	Control over treatment	Study designs	Possible uses
Experimental or interventional	Yes	Randomize	A/B testing, trials, knockouts
Non-experimental or observational	No	Cohort Case-control Surveys	CLV ML, AI NPS

11.3 Statistical population and subpopulations

In previous sections, we introduced *qualitative* and *quantitative* variables, the statistics that apply to each variable type, and the concept of *experimental design*. Now we define the notion of *statistical population* because the population that statistics are estimated from determine how they are interpreted.

A *statistical population* is a set of similar items of interest for a question or experiment [17]. Here we further define a population as an ensemble of online payments that share a common characteristic.

In the case of the Observatory for Payment Card Security (OSCP) published by the Banque de France [8], the common characteristic is the country; the report describes payment fraud in the set of online payments acquired by French acquiring services or processed by French issuers.

Another population is the set of online payments made on an e-commerce service. In that case, fraud is considered within the sales of that merchant. For example, a subpopulation would be all the sales made via a PayPal payment.

Previous examples are instances of dynamic populations, where actual cardholders making purchases change over time. Alternatively, fixed populations are also possible; notably, this could be the case if an e-commerce service distributes coupons to a determined set of VIP clients.

11.4 Sources of identified frauds and fraud subtypes

After having introduced a *statistical population*, we determine several payment frauds subtypes. The following table summarizes the five subtypes of fraud a large merchant could face.

Sources of identified fraud
Frauds are detected during acquisition or after

Timing	#	Fraud reason
Stopped by	1	Card is blacklisted.
acquirer	2	Other failure reasons that suggest a fraud.
After	3	3D Secure-enabled but reported as fraud.
payment	4	A chargeback for fraud reason has escalated.
acquisition	5	Risk analysts have labeled it as a fraud.

Hence, measurements of fraud for online payments will factor in those five subtypes. However, not all five subtypes will always be available for each considered population.

Finally, we formally define payment fraud as an event Y and $P(Y)$ its probability of occurring in the *statistical population* called: Total sales amount (or number).

Estimating payment fraud
Fraud sales over total sales in population per period

$$P(Y) = \frac{\text{Sale's amount (or number) of fraud}}{\text{Total sales amount (or number)}} \qquad (11.1)$$

Given a population, e.g., a country or a merchant; and a period, e.g., a year or the last 30 days.

11.5 Data types and experimental design: Key points

In brief

Different data types exist, including qualitative and quantitative variables. Qualitative variables are either nominal or ordinal. Quantitative variables are intervals or ratio.

Because it is not possible to estimate parameters such as averages or standard deviations on qualitative variables, the set of statistical methods that apply to them are called non-parametric.

The two main types of studies are experimental and non-experimental. The former influences the treatment (such as the randomization for A/B testing), and the latter does not.

For non-experimental studies, the three main types of designs are cohort, where members of a group are followed over time; case control, where the relationship between the variables and the phenomenon is analyzed; and surveys, which measure a phenomenon at one point in time.

Five sources of fraud identification have been described, e.g., if the payment card hits a blacklist on the side of the acquirer or if the risk operation analyst classified the payment as a fraud. Taken together, these sources of fraud identification help define the sub-population of fraud.

Key points

- A variable tracks changes over time in values associated with a quality or quantity of interest.

11.5 Data types and experimental design: Key points

- *Non-parametric* statistical methods apply to variables that are nominal or ordinal.

- *Parametric* statistical methods apply to variables that are intervals or ratios.

- *Experimental* studies influence the treatment. They are used for *A/B testing*, i.e., randomization.

- Non-experimental studies do not influence the treatment. They are descriptive and/or analytic.

- The customer lifetime value (CLV) is measured using cohort design.

- Machine learning (ML) and artificial intelligence (AI) models are usually built using case-control design (e.g., fraud or not fraud).

- The net promoter score (NPS) is measured using *surveys*.

- Estimation of statistics requires clearly defining populations and subpopulations.

- Not all sources of identified fraud materialize as charge-backs, but statistical models tend to include all fraud subtypes as one fraud class.

12   Essential methods to measure risk and test hypotheses

Background   The previous chapter provided the necessary foundations for data analysis. We described the concept of variables, the statistical methods applicable to each variable subtype, various experimental designs, and the two types of errors a model can make. However, more methods and concepts are still necessary to derive meaningful conclusions from data.

Problem   Notably, the data may have *missing values*. How do we deal with them? Furthermore, the data may not be in the best format. How do we *transform* it? Finally, some variables are quantitative but others are qualitative. What statistical methods apply to each variable type? These are the questions we will address in this chapter.

12.1 Measuring data and mixing in additional information

When clients buy products from e-commerce services, specific information describing the purchase is saved in the merchant's IT system, such as:

- the amount value of the sale, e.g., $24.12;

- the products or services bought, e.g., "yellow t-shirt";

- the payment method used to make the purchase, e.g., "Visa";

- the client's email addresses, e.g., "abc@hotmail.com"; and

- the delivery address, e.g., "123 1st St., New York, NY 10010".

Before attempting to interpret the information, this data must be processed and converted into a format that is more suitable for data analysis. For instance:

- Addresses must be geocoded to obtain the latitude, longitude, and other geographical information;

- Text must be transformed into matrices of numbers; and

- Amounts in different currencies must be converted to a single currency, e.g., USD or EUR.

12.2 Dealing with missing values

The resulting data may contain missing values [104], which will cause problems because most statistical methods do not handle them well.

Data may be missing for various reasons. Some of these reasons are *random*, while others are not. Several possible causes for missing values are reported in the following table.

Reasons for missing values

Improper data entry or collection may lead to missing values

#	Reasons
1	The data entry is improperly done.
2	The client did not provide the information.
3	The acquiring service did not provide the information.
4	The internal data processing failed to keep the information.

If the data are missing due to a programming error, the error is systematic and, therefore, not random. Fixing it and re-processing the data may address the issue. However, many times this is not feasible because the data is not recoverable; in these cases, the missing data must be managed.

The traditional ways to manage missing values are as follows:

- drop the cases that have missing information;

- impute the missing value with the average [96];

- impute the missing values with expectation-maximization [9];

- carry out multiple imputation.

12.3 Transforming the data

Once data are available as matrices of numbers where no data are missing anymore, data transformations are commonly applied [79]. Some common transformations are reported in the following table.

Transforming the measured values
To remove scale effect, extract information, or re-calibrate

Name	Formula	Description
Center	$x - \tilde{x}$	To bring the expected mean values back to zero.
Scale	$\frac{x}{f(x)}$ with $f \in \{\sigma, \max, ...\}$	To remove the effect of the scale.
Recalibrate	$f(x)$ with $f \in \{ln, \sqrt{\cdot}, e, ...\}$	To emphasize, e.g., small or large values.
Normalize	$\frac{x - \tilde{x}}{f(x)}$ with $f \in \{\sigma, \max, ...\}$	To center and bring values onto comparable scales.
Indicator	$\delta_{x,y} = \begin{cases} 1, & \text{if } x = y. \\ 0, & \text{otherwise.} \end{cases}$	To extract a single level or value from a variable.
Quantile	$P(X < x)$	To disregard value differences but keep order.
Tf-idf	Each word's contribution is weighted as a function of the term frequency (tf) and its inverse frequency in all text documents (idf) [127].	

The transformed numbers compose the set of predictor (or independent) variables [81], which statistical methods rely upon to build statistical models.

12.4 Measuring fraud prevalence and incidence

To study how frequently a phenomenon, such as payment fraud, occurs in a population, two types of rates exist: the *prevalence* and the *incidence*.

The two rates are calculated with the same formula, but the time range changes; the formula is reported below.

Prevalence and incidence of fraud
Same formula; different time horizons

$$P(Y|\delta t) = \frac{N(Y|\delta t)}{N} \qquad (12.1)$$

where δt is,   e.g., one year or seven days;
$N(Y|\delta t)$ is   the number of new cases of fraud;
N is   the size of the population at risk.

$$\textbf{Incidence} = P(Y|\delta t) \qquad (12.2)$$
$$\textbf{Prevalence} = P(Y) = lim_{\delta t \to \infty} P(Y|\delta t) \qquad (12.3)$$

However, distinguishing between the prevalence and the incidence is not always easy. For this reason, below we work out an example factoring the time dimension in the fraud rate. Depending on the time horizon, the measure is either an incidence rate or the prevalence of fraud.

If we assume a prevalence of payment fraud of 0.8% for online payments in France [8], the incidence rate of payment fraud within the four weeks after a sale is, on average, 0.4%. However, after six months, the incidence is 0.8%, i.e., the prevalence of fraud in France.

Distinguishing prevalence from incidence
Four weeks after a payment, incidence of fraud is 0.4%

Because it usually takes one month to escalate a payment fraud case (cf. escalation time described previously), only half (50%) of all payment fraud cases are escalated after the first four weeks. This also means that half (50%) of the cases are not escalated, which illustrates how incidence varies with the time range considered.

12.5 Contingency tables

The statistical methods used to analyze quantitative variables and qualitative variables are different. In the coming sections, we review the methods that apply to *qualitative variables*.

In particular, here we introduce *contingency tables*, which represent the distribution of two qualitative variables in a matrix format.

To give an example, a contingency table could analyze the *joint distribution* of the country code of the IP address, e.g., GB, with the fraud status. The following table illustrates such an example.

12.6 Odd ratios

To further summarize the previous contingency table, odds ratios (OR) are frequently used. ORs measure how strongly the presence of the qualitative attribute, e.g., GB as the IP country code, is associated with the phenomenon, i.e., payment fraud.

Two-ways contingency table
Joint and marginal distributions of two categorical variables

IP country code	Fraud status					Totals
	Fraud			Not fraud		
GB	9.1%	**300** 0.1% 23.0%	0.3%		**1,000** 0.3% 77.0%	**1,300** 0.4% 100.0%
Not GB	90.9%	**3,000** 1.0% 1.0%	99.7%	**300,000** 98.6% 99.0%		**303,000** 99.6% 100.0%
Totals	100.0%	**3,300** 1.1%	100.0%	**301,000** 98.9%		**304,300** 100.0%

Sources: Ubivar.com client (values are rounded)

ORs are calculated as follows:

$$OR = \frac{\frac{\text{Number of cases with the attribute}}{\text{Number of cases}}}{\frac{\text{Number of non-cases with the attribute}}{\text{Number of non-cases}}} \qquad (12.4)$$

For example, the OR for the previous contingency table is:

$$OR = \frac{\frac{300}{3,300}}{\frac{1,000}{300,000}} = \frac{9.1\%}{0.3\%} = 30 \qquad (12.5)$$

In the following table we explain how to interpret odd ratios.

12.7 Confidence intervals of odd ratios

Confidence intervals [70] help measure the interval of estimates given their statistical distribution. For the OR, it is estimated from the cell counts (cf. table below), the natural logarithm of the odd

Understanding odd ratios
OR compares attribute frequencies in population with frauds

> An OR of 30 for GB as the IP country code on this e-commerce
> service means that in the population of fraudulent payments, the
> likelihood of having an IP address whose country code is GB
> (9.1%) is 30 times greater than that in the normal population of
> non-fraudulent buyers (0.3%).

ratio ($\ln OR$), and the z-value of the normal distribution at the
level α—we define z-values in a latter section, when we examine
confidence intervals for quantitative variables.

Confidence intervals for odd ratios
Confidence intervals depend on the cell counts: a, b, c, d

IP country code	Fraud status	
	Fraud	Not fraud
GB	a	b
Not GB	c	d

Sources: Ubivar.com client (values are rounded)

The sequence of steps to calculate the confidence interval is as follows:

$$se\,(\ln OR) = \sqrt{\frac{1}{a} + \frac{1}{b} + \frac{1}{c} + \frac{1}{d}} \qquad (12.6)$$

$$CI_\alpha\,[\ln OR] = \ln OR \pm z_{\frac{\alpha}{2}} \times se\,(\ln OR) \qquad (12.7)$$

$$CI_\alpha\,[OR] = e^{CI_\alpha[\ln OR]} \qquad (12.8)$$

For the $OR = 30$, the confidence interval is:

$$se\,(\ln OR) = \sqrt{\frac{1}{300} + \frac{1}{1000} + \frac{1}{3000} + \frac{1}{300000}} \qquad (12.9)$$

$$se\,(\ln OR) = 0.07 \qquad (12.10)$$

$$CI_{2.5\%}\,[OR] = e^{3.40 - 1.96 \times 0.07} = 26.1 \qquad (12.11)$$

$$CI_{97.5\%}\,[OR] = e^{3.40 + 1.96 \times 0.07} = 34.4 \qquad (12.12)$$

There is a 95% chance that the OR will be between 26.15 and 34.41[1].

12.8 Hypothesis testing

In previous sections we introduced *contingency tables* and we summarize them with *odd ratios*. However, it is frequently the case that two qualitative attributes have similar ORs, e.g., 2 and 2.1. To differentiate between the two, statistical *tests* are used [125].

These *tests* aim to measure the likelihood that statistics, e.g., an OR of 2 or a difference of 0.1 between two ORs (2.1–2.0), would be measured purely by chance, i.e., at random. These tests return a value between 0 (0%) and 1 (100%) called the p-value, where p is the probability (or the likelihood).

Various tests exist for qualitative variables, e.g., the χ^2-test (chi square) [65] and the Fisher's exact test [87], which measure association, or the goodness of fit test [94].

---

[1]Because the confidence interval of the OR does not contain 1, we reject the null hypothesis of an absence of association between the exposure (GB, not GB) and the fraud status. Therefore, there is an association.

Quantifying the strength of an association

A zip code highly associated with fraud: $OR = 138, p = 5e^{-9}$

		Fraud status	
		Fraud	Not fraud
Postal	FR-99999	5	21
Code	Not FR-99999	7	4,135

Sources: Ubivar.com client (zip code value obfuscated)

With the previous contingency table, a χ^2-test returns $p = 0.0005$, and Fisher's exact test returns $p = 4.8e - 09$ ($p = 0.0000000048$), which is very small; in other words, it is unlikely that the distribution of counts in this contingency table would occur simply by chance alone.

Null and alternative hypotheses

To reject the null is to accept the alternative hypothesis

Statistics uses the term of null hypothesis (H_0) to refer to the likelihood that a statistics or a series of measurements would be observed by chance alone.

Then, if the statistical test's p-value is lower than, e.g., 5%, the null hypothesis H_0 would be rejected at a significance level $\alpha = 5\%$ and the alternative hypothesis H_1 should be accepted.

In the case of the count data reported previously, because the p-value is so small ($p = 4.8e - 09$), we reject H_0 and we must accept the alternative hypothesis (H_1), i.e., the presence of an association.

12.9 Central tendency

In previous sections, we described the statistical method used to describe and infer results from qualitative variables. Here we review the methods that apply to quantitative variables. We will cover the mean, the median, and the standard deviation. Then, we discuss why it is important to estimate these statistics. Finally, we examine confidence intervals for quantitative variables.

The mean [102] and the median [103] are two statistical measures of the central tendency of a quantitative variable. For instance, with the series of numbers $1, 2, 3, 4, 20$, the number 3 is the median and the mean (or average) is 6.

The median is defined as the number at the midpoint of the frequency distribution (the series above) of observed values or quantities [103]; there is an equal probability (50%) of falling on the left or right of that number. On the other hand, the mean [102] is the sum of the values divided by the number of values.

Where X is the observed value and n is the number of observations, the mean is expressed as follows:

$$\mu = \frac{\Sigma X}{n}$$
(12.13)

12.10 Dispersion

Then, the standard deviation is a measure of the dispersion of the measurements of a quantitative variable.

For an e-commerce service based in the UK and selling primarily in the UK, most of the sales will be concentrated in London (the geographical center), while the rest of the sales will be dispersed in the rest of the country and abroad.

The standard deviation is estimated as follows:

$$\sigma = \sqrt{\frac{\Sigma\left(X - \mu\right)^2}{n - 1}} \tag{12.14}$$

The square of the standard deviation (σ^2) is called the variance.

12.11 Standard normal

Estimating the mean and the standard deviation matters because parametric distributions can be represented abstractly and thus summarize the quantitative variable.

Distributions, such as the normal [108] or the χ^2 distributions [65], are also used to estimate confidence intervals and carry out statistical inference.

The probability density function $f(x|\mu, \sigma^2)$ of the standard normal, i.e., the probability that a value fall within a particular range of the distribution, is defined as follows:

$$f(x|\mu, \sigma^2) = \frac{1}{\sqrt{2\pi\sigma^2}} e^{-\frac{(x-\mu)^2}{2\sigma^2}} \tag{12.15}$$

12.12 Confidence intervals

When observed values follow a normal distribution, e.g., with distances or proportions (when these are not too close to 0 or 1), the confidence interval (CI) is calculated as follows:

$$CI_\alpha = \frac{\mu \pm z \times \sigma}{\sqrt{n}} \tag{12.16}$$

where z-scores are derived from the normal distribution [108]. When building confidence intervals, e.g., 95% or 99%, z-score values are usually picked directly from tables; below we report three commonly used z-score values.

Typical z-scores of the normal distribution
Two-sided significance levels to build confidence intervals

Confidence interval	From	To	z-score
95%	2.5%	97.5%	1.960
98%	1.0%	99.0%	2.326
99%	0.5%	99.5%	2.576

To further illustrate the concept of confidence interval, in the following figure we report the relation between the probability density function, the z-values, and the proportion of data that is within the upper and lower bounds at 95%, 98%, and 99%.

Probability density function of the normal
95% of the distribution is within two standard deviations

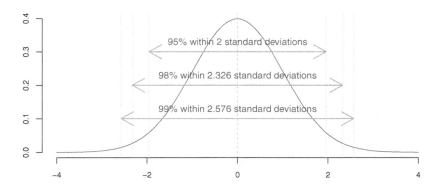

12.13 Essential methods to measure risk and test hypotheses: Key points

In brief

An e-commerce service *collects* different data during a customer's purchase. This data is often *complemented* with additional information. Later, data is *transformed*.

The reasons why some *values are missing* should be investigated. Many times, missingness is not random. Missingness should be fixed whenever possible; alternatively, *imputation* methods exist.

Contingency tables are then used to analyze qualitative variables. Notably, *odd ratios* measure the strength of an association between an attribute value and fraud.

Finally, we mentioned the *mean, median, standard deviation, confidence intervals*, and *z-scores*, which are statistics describing quantitative variables.

Key points

- Data is *collected, complemented* with additional information, and *transformed*.

- In most cases, values are not missing at random. Therefore, it is important to understand why they are missing and fix the reason.

- Data transformations help reduce differences in centers and scales between variables. They also improve the calibration of the measurements.

- *Contingency tables* help estimate the accuracy and errors made by prediction models.

- *Prevalence* measures the proportion of fraud at one point in time.

- *Incidence* measures the proportion of new cases of fraud over a period of time.

- *Odds ratios* measure how strongly the presence of a qualitative attribute is associated with fraud.

- *P-values* estimate the likelihood that statistics like the χ^2-score, an odd ratio, or a difference in mean are measured by chance alone.

- A *confidence interval* corresponds to the chances (e.g., 95%) that the true statistical estimate is between the provided lower and upper bound.

- In many situations, confidence intervals are derived from the *normal* distribution and its z-statistic.

13 | Teaching machines to predict

Background The previous two chapters laid the necessary foundations for data analyses to occur. They described a set of essential statistical methods to measure risk and test hypotheses.

Problem In this chapter, we consider the process of training machines to predict a phenomenon such as payment fraud in e-commerce services.

13.1 Problem dimension: 1D, 2D, 3D, ... 1,000,000D!

The dimension of a space is the minimum number of coordinates needed to specify any point within it [82, 131].

For instance, any point on a sheet of paper could be specified in terms of its coordinates along each side of the sheet. Here the dimension would be two. An instance of space with three dimensions would be a geospatial environment in which height is added. There would be four dimensions if we add time.

In e-commerce services, some examples of dimensions could include the following:

- the amount of the order;
- how often the client has visited the website;
- how long it took the client to make the actual payment;
- whether the client ordered a t-shirt; or
- whether the client is a repeat customer.

In mathematics, each dimension represents a *vector* [18]; together, the set of vectors represents the *basis* of a vector space. For e-commerce services, we gave five possible dimensions, but there could be tens of thousands of dimensions or even millions!

The number of dimensions is called the *cardinality* [18] of the basis or, more commonly, the dimension of the problem. Moreover, the process of converting the information collected, e.g., a client's purchases online, to a vector space is called a *projection* [118] or a map to a vector space representation.

The set of clients who made purchases on the e-commerce service is called the *data set* [78]. Each client is called a *data point* [76].

In mathematics, a data set is represented as a data *matrix* or just a matrix [18], i.e., a rectangular array composed of numbers where the number of rows corresponds to the number of data points and the number of columns is the dimension of the vector space.

In previous chapters, we called attention to the problem of missing values because most statistical methods do not deal well with missing values. Therefore, in the rest of this chapter, we assume that there are no missing values after the data has been prepared.

Assumption   Henceforth, we assume that there are no missing values in the analyzed data matrices.

13.2 Reducing dimension: The purpose

The previous section introduced the concepts of data sets, data matrices, and projection onto a vector space representation. One challenge, however, is that not all the dimensions of the vector space are useful. For instance, some of the dimensions are made of identical values, while other dimensions observe random or unrelated values.

To address this problem, data reduction [77], dimensionality reduction [83], and/or feature selection [14] are frequently used. These methods help to reduce *sparsity*; reduce *collinearity*; *select dimensions*; and prevent *overfitting*.

Reduce   Some methods help reduce the number of
sparsity   zero-elements in a matrix [124].

Reduce collinearity	Other methods help reduce collinearity between dimensions of the vector space [106], which occurs when, e.g., two dimensions measure the same thing and one is, therefore, redundant.
Select dimensions	Additional methods help identify the dimensions [14] that are the most highly related to the phenomenon measured, e.g., fraud.
Prevent overfitting	Finally, some methods are designed to prevent overfitting [20] when attempting to teach machines how to predict a concept based on a vector of observations.

13.3 Reducing dimension: Methods

Reducing the size of the data matrices is a core concept in statistical modeling. A wide range of methods have been developed; some apply to specific domains, some are generic, and some are integrated with statistical learning algorithms, which embed some of these methods within their algorithms.

In the following table we summarize two classes of vector space reduction methods as well as their different types, subtypes, and name.

Vector space reduction methods

PCA, R^2, χ^2, and lasso are commonly used

Class	Type	Subtype	Name
Matrix rotation	Orthogonal transform		PCA
Feature selection	Filter	Correlation	R^2
		Association	χ^2
		Entropy	Information gain
	Wrapper	Stepwise regression	Forward
			Backward
	Embedded	Classification	l_1-SVM
		Regression	Lasso

Sources: more information on these methods is available in [14, 117, 25, 19, 97]

Below, we describe and provide references for the different vector space reduction methods, i.e., *PCA*, R^2, χ^2, *wrapper* methods, and *embedded feature selection methods.*

PCA   This method converts a set of possible related observations into a set of linearly uncorrelated vectors called principal components [117].

PCA is commonly used to feed an orthogonal matrix to a statistical modeling algorithm.

R^2, χ^2, **information gain**   These methods are examples of statistics commonly used to filter out irrelevant dimensions.

Wrapper methods   These methods [25], such as *stepwise forward* and *backward* regression, are other approaches used to select a combined set of dimensions.

Embedded feature selection   Two examples of embedded feature selection methods are lasso and l_1-SVM.

13.4 Statistical learning: Methods

Statistical methods, particularly those that focus on teaching machines how to learn concepts, are based on algorithms, i.e., step-by-step procedures that take input values, like numbers, and that yield an output value like a payment fraud risk score (%) or a class (fraud, not fraud), in a finite number of steps [53, 52].

In *statistical learning*, two notable subtypes of algorithms are used, i.e., *supervised algorithms* and *unsupervised algorithms* [20].

Supervised   Supervised algorithms are designed to learn classification problems with two or more classes.

Identifying payment fraud is an instance of a *binary* task [15], but multi-class problems also exist.

Optical character recognition [110] is an instance of *multiclass* problem. Taxonomic multi-class prediction is another, e.g., when posting on a classified website like eBay, product categories are automatically proposed given the title.

There are also sets of regression methods [20]; some of which can, in turn, be used for classification.

Unsupervised There are also algorithms that focus on unsupervised tasks. These algorithms exist to identify structure in data, i.e., groups or clusters [10] of data points that share common characteristics.

This is especially useful when a complex phenomenon, e.g., payment fraud or a complex pathology like Parkinson's disease, is broken down into a set of simpler and more homogeneous subtypes.

In the following table, we list some of the methods commonly used in statistical learning to address each problem.

Statistical learning methods

Common supervised and unsupervised algorithms

Type	Name	Classification algorithm(s)
Supervised	SVM	One vs. one and one vs. all
	Naive Bayes	Most likely class
	k-NN	Most common class
	Decision trees	Default to multi-class
	Random forest	
	Neural networks (deep learning)	Cutoff (e.g., 50%), one vs. all and most likely class
	Logistic and lasso regression	
Unsupervised	K-means	
	Model-based clustering	

Sources: more information on these methods is available in [80, 3, 7, 10, 15, 20, 27]

13.5 Preventing overfitting: Regularization methods

To verify how well statistical learning machines have learned a phenomenon, a step called model evaluation is carried out. This aims to evaluate whether the model (the mathematical abstraction learned from specific instances) can generalize well.

A model may not generalize well if it overfits the data [20], which occurs when the model becomes sensitive to the noise in the data set. Below, we illustrate on a concrete example the concept of *model overfitting*.

Model overfitting
Learning word-by-word and not the general concepts

> A practical example of overfitting would be that of a student who tries very hard to learn every words in a textbook by heart but who fails to pick up the general concepts taught by the textbook.

To prevent *overfitting*, two common techniques involve penalizing models for their complexity, which is also called *regularization* [120] and *test set*, which we see in the next section.

Regularization   Instead of optimizing an objective function that simply measures how accurate the model is, e.g., via the likelihood or the accuracy, a regularized objective function has a penalty parameter that is proportional to the model complexity.

Two instances of regularized methods are the *ridge regression* (norm l2) and the *lasso* (norm l1) [20].

The formula below describes a regularized objective function with a penalty parameter, whose importance is determined by λ.

Regularization
Penalizing for model complexity

Optimize: Cost for errors $+ \lambda \times$ Model complexity   (13.1)

13.6 Preventing overfitting: Training and test set

We first described regularization as a strategy to reduce overfitting. Now, we introduce the alternative approach, which is to evaluate the model on a *test set* [20].

Test set The test set approach is, in practice, made of (at least) two sets of data points: the *test set* and the *training set*.

First, the points from the *training set* are used to fit the statistical model.

Second, the (previously unseen) points in the *test set* are used to evaluate the performance of the model.

In practice, the process of evaluating the model's performance is often done several times. Various methods to split the training and test set exist, such as the *holdout*, *cross-validation*, and *jackknife* (or hold one out) methods.

Holdout This method simply creates 5, 7, 10, or more training and test set partitions of the data set at random. The measure of the model performance is then repeated over each training and test set split. The average performance is reported with its confidence interval.

Cross-validation   In contrast to the holdout method, which splits in two, the cross-validation method splits data sets in 5, 7, 10 or more partitions of the data set. Then, the model is iteratively trained on all but one partition; the left-out partition is rotated. The average performance is also reported with its confidence interval.

Jackknife or hold one out   Finally, the jackknife or hold-one-out method is an extension of the cross-validation method, where the number of partitions is the number of data points in the data set.
    In turn, this means that each test set is composed of only one data point and that the rotation will occur as many times as there are data points.

13.7 Handling class imbalance: Sampling strategies

Often, the modeled phenomenon is rare, e.g., on average, 0.8% of all payments are considered as fraudulent in France. In this case, it is said the problem has a strong class imbalance.

Hence, when evaluating how the model generalizes with the holdout or cross validation method, some partitions of the training and test set will have different proportions (%) of data points per class.

To reduce the influence of differences due to the sampling and the class imbalance, various approaches exist. Below, we mention three approaches: *stratified sampling*, *under sampling*, and *over sampling.*

Stratified sampling

One approach is to partition the holdout and cross-validation so each class is represented with stable proportions in each training/test-set split.

This is called stratified sampling. The benefit of this approach is that the variation due to the differing class proportion in each partition is minimized.

Under sampling

Another approach is to reduce the total size of the learning problem by undersampling the most prevalent class [8].

However, in that case the class priors [9], i.e., the probability of each class, are changed. Therefore, to have predicted values on the same scale as that of the analyzed population, it is necessary to adjust the final estimates of the model trained on the subpopulation.

Over sampling

Finally, the counterpart of undersampling is called oversampling [8]. In that case, data points are selected that can potentially be picked more than one time; these sampling methods are called with replacement.

One instance is bootstrapping [10]. Its main use is to estimate the sampling distribution of almost any (performance) statistics, which is necessary to estimate the confidence interval.

13.8 Validating models: Contingency table

To measure the *performance* of a statistical model, namely its abilities to generalize, a *contingency table* is usually built. In the case of payment fraud, since payments either are fraudulent or are not, and since the statistical algorithm predicts whether the data point is fraud, there are four possible cases.

Depending on the combination of the real class and the prediction, the contingency table counts the number of true positives and true negatives (accurate predictions), and the number of false positives and negatives (errors).

The table below describes a contingency table summarizing the number of cases accurately and erroneously classified.

Contingency table
Summarizing the performance of a model

		Prediction	
		Fraud	Not fraud
Reality	Fraud	True positive (TP)	False negative (FN)
	Not fraud	False positive (FP)	True negative (TN)

13.9 Validating models: Performance measures

To evaluate the *generalization* of the statistical model, an array of *performance* measures exists, many of which are based on the contingency table.

These metrics include accuracy, sensitivity, specificity, precision, recall, F-measures, and area under the curve (AUC). Though, likelihood-based and correlation-based metrics also exist like the Akaike information criterion (AIC) and Bayesian information criterion (BIC), which derive from the likelihood, and the R^2, a correlation measure between the prediction and the class.

The different performance metrics to summarize the performance of a model are summarized in the table below.

Performance metrics
Summarizing the performance of a model

Based on	Name	Formula	Description
Contingency table	Accuracy	$\frac{TP+TN}{n}$	Correct classifications
	Error	$\frac{FP+FN}{n}$	Incorrect classifications
	Sensitivity	$\frac{TP}{TP+FN}$	Likelihood of detecting the positive class
	Specificity	$\frac{TN}{FP+TN}$	Likelihood of detecting the negative class
	Precision	$\frac{TP}{TP+FP}$	Likelihood that positive predictions are correct
	Recall	$\frac{TN}{TN+FN}$	Likelihood that negative predictions are correct
Precision (P) and recall (R)	AUC		Area under the curve
	F	$\frac{(1+\beta^2)\times P\times R}{R+\beta^2\times P}$	Weighted harmonic mean of precision and recall
Likelihood	AIC	$2k-2ln(\hat{L})$	
	BIC	$k\times ln(n)-2ln(\hat{L})$	Weighted harmonic mean of precision and recall
Prediction score	R^2		Spearman correlation between predictor and class

Sources: see [71, 119, 51, 58, 41]

13.10 Teaching machines to predict: Key points

In brief

Points of mathematical problems are positioned in a vector space in terms of coordinates. Often, today's problems consider tens or even hundreds of thousands of dimensions for inclusion in a model.

Because of the collinearity between the dimensions and the danger that statistical algorithms overfit the data, dimension reduction is often carried out by matrix rotation or feature selection, which are either filter, wrapper, or embedded methods.

Support Vector Machines (SVM), k nearest neighbors (k-NN), neural networks (deep learning), and regression methods produce classification or regression functions. They are instances of supervised statistical learning algorithms.

K-means and model-based clustering, which intend to identify structures in data, are instances of unsupervised statistical learning algorithms.

The model evaluation process aims to assess whether the trained statistical model can generalize. Often, model validation and performance evaluation is carried out by fitting a statistical model on a training set and evaluating its performance on a test set.

The strategies used to partition the data in a training and test set may be the holdout, cross-validation, and jackknife methods; they may also involve various sampling mechanisms, e.g., undersampling the prevalent class, stratified sampling, and bootstrapping.

Finally, many different performance measures exist; each catches part of the performance.

Key points

- A *dimension* of a space is the minimum number of coordinates needed to specify any point within it.

- The set of clients who made purchases on the e-commerce service is called the *data set*.

- *Dimension reduction* is often carried out to reduce collinearity between the dimensions and to prevent *overfitting*.

- *Matrix rotation* and *feature selection* are two common strategies to reduce dimension.

- Model validation is the process of verifying the machine's predictions.

- *Regularization* is a technique to penalize statistical models for the increase in complexity, thereby preventing overfitting.

- Often, the data set is split into a train set, which is used to learn the statistical model, and a test set, which is used to evaluate the model.

- Holdout, cross-validation, and jackknife methods are used to repeat the model performance estimation and average the result.

- Stratified, undersampling, and oversampling are strategies used to control the train and test set, especially if there is a class imbalance.

V | Towards risk management intelligence

Background

In the first part of this book, we reviewed the different intermediaries that make online payments possible, reviewed some payment methods that are commonly used to pay online, and described the online payment process.

Then we looked at why things may go wrong when processing payments online; how things go wrong, notably when payment fraud is committed; and the factors that influence the occurrence of payment fraud.

Next, we reviewed the range of solutions to prevent payment fraud, provided a bird's-eye view of the payment fraud prevention process, looked at the bits and pieces of fraud detection, and described the fraud prevention auditing process.

In the previous part, we reviewed the preliminary conditions to carry out data analyses to prevent fraud, described the essential statistical methods to measure risk and test hypotheses, and reviewed how to teach machines to predict a concept like payment fraud.

Problem

In this part, we review the application of corporate financial risk management methods to prevent, detect, and manage fraud prevention for e-commerce services.

Outline

First, we review ideal fraud detection systems for e-commerce services. Second, we describe risk classification, the concept of escalation time, and risk ratings. Finally, we propose the application of the concept of value at risk (VAR) to pilot risk in e-commerce services.

14   Ideal fraud detection: The north star

Background   It is often useful to reflect on the essential features of an *ideal* system because it provides a framework against which we can measure progress and make comparisons.

Problem   Therefore, we define the ideal fraud prevention system and, when the ideal solution is impractical, define an ideal and practical solution.

14.1 Detect 100% of payment fraud

There are various methods of incurring absolutely no payment fraud. Below, we describe three approaches, i.e., to accept *no payments* at all; to accept only payments that bear no fraud risk; and to adopt a *practically ideal* solution.

No more payments

Cutting all inflow of payments is the most obvious (and most impractical, in most cases) way of stopping all payment fraud. While it seems silly to mention it, it can be useful to have this corner-case laid out. When payment fraud spins out of control in an e-commerce service, the ultimate option is to close the valve.

A tradeoff is to restrict aggressively the range of payments accepted. In this case, the valves of the revenue machine are still open, but less so.

Risk-free payment methods

Alternatively, e-commerce services may decide to limit the payment methods accepted to those that are risk-free.

Risk-free payment methods tend to be those in which the customer pushes the money to the merchant, e.g., direct banking, International Bank Account Number (IBAN), or wire transfers, which is the opposite of payment methods that pull funds like payment cards.

However, direct banking, IBAN, or wire transfers are not yet as available as payment cards. In addition, the design of their authentication mechanisms is likely to limit one-click checkout, which is known to simplify and boost conversion.

Ideal and practical solution
The ideal and practical fraud detection solution does not detect 100% of all fraud attempts.

However, it dynamically optimizes the cost benefit of letting through fraudsters and rejecting real clients. We will go into more detail in the next chapter.

14.2 Never reject any real customer

When a merchant receives a payment authorization from a client, it engages the order fulfilment process. However, the merchant is uncertain about the future outcome of the payment. There is a risk of failure. Hence, to make sure all true clients get their orders fulfilled, the merchant needs to have full trust in its clients.

Previously, we covered several pathways to raise the level of trust. Among those there are engineering of trust, payments methods with two-factor authentication, and unfalsifiable proofs of address or identity.

Engineering trust	Trust may be engineered by suggesting that clients link their social media accounts and verifying the client's phone number and email address.
Two-factor authentica-tion	Another option is to switch to push payments or to 3D Secure. However, those approaches tend to reduce checkout velocity and conversion.
Requesting unfalsifiable documents	Finally, merchants may request unfalsifiable proofs of address or identity, e.g., signed QR codes such as 2D-Doc [1]. However, the request process by definition also reduces checkout velocity and conver-sion, but also buying satisfaction.

14.3 No software: Core and non-core features

To build trust with their clients and partners and to be seen as re-liable, merchants need to operate their service 365 days per year, seven days a week, and 24 hours a day. Therefore, one of the goals of e-commerce services is to prevent software bugs.

However, bugs are inevitable in the process of developing new software features. For example, bugs may happen when an e-commerce platform is upgraded and the plugin does not support the new version.

More generally, the further away the software components are from the *core* programs, the less these programs are tested and the more likely it is that bugs will occur. In fact, software platforms for e-commerce, e.g., Magento, PrestaShop, and WooCommerce, have *core* and *non-core* features.

Non-core features   Non-core features are developed by the core team or by external software vendors. These non-core features are often plugins, i.e., software components that add a specific feature to an existing computer program [116].

14.4 No software: The subscription model

Currently, the software industry is still moving to the software as a service (SaaS) business model, i.e., the subscription economy. For merchants, the primary drivers of this move are *lower upfront investments*, *cost-effectiveness*, *increased reliability* and *performance*, and the *absence of maintenance*.

Low upfront investment   The initial investment to get a working e-commerce service is lower.

Cost effectiveness   Compared to self-managed software stacks that demand expertise and funds to operate, SaaS software is more cost-effective.

Reliability and performance   By pooling resources across all clients, SaaS vendors build up their expertise and add layers of redundancy designed to improve reliability and performance.

Absence of   The SaaS provider maintains the software in
maintenance   an evergreen state; the beneficiary of the SaaS
                         solution does not need to maintain it.

The SaaS model therefore has the advantages of the lower upfront investments, cost effectiveness, reliability, and performance.

14.5 No software: Fraud Prevention as a Service

It is also common that e-commerce services manage part of the e-commerce software stack and just rely on dedicated SaaS vendors for special functions of the e-commerce service. If merchants manage the core of their e-commerce service and need a fraud risk prevention system, then the two traditional approaches are to integrate directly with *APIs* or to *install a plugin*, and a third approach is to do *without any plugin*.

API   When merchants integrate with APIs [55],
Integration   merchants can customize functionalities.
                         However, the burden of the implementation
                         rests on their shoulders.

Plugin   When merchants decide to install a standard
installation   plugin, then they run the risk of incompati-
                         bilities during software upgrade, which may
                         lead to the downtime of their service.

Plugin-free   To address this issue, a third alternative has emerged amongst SaaS vendors, i.e., to just integrate without having to install any software.

In a context other than fraud, Yodlee [134] integrates with banks, helping SaaS accounting software vendors obtain accounting information from banks worldwide.

14.6 Immediate response time

Another challenge for e-commerce services involves responding rapidly to online orders. The payer, who authorizes a payment and expects products to get delivered, and the payee, who enters a commercial contract that involves trust.

However, a fast response time also matters when managing risk, e.g., when fraud is detected. If the delay is too long between acquiring the payment and finishing the payment verification, this may cause *settlement*, *operational*, and *commercial* risks.

Settlement   The price of the product or service may have changed, especially if it is volatile, e.g., the price of an airline ticket.

Operational   The e-commerce service may have already fulfilled the order and expedited the products.

Commercial   First, the e-commerce service may not fulfill its commercial contract, e.g., pay online and pick up in two hours.

Second, clients may not appreciate processing delays that are too long; this will negatively influence their overall satisfaction.

Ideally, the response time for risk management, e.g., as applied to fraud detection, should be immediate because of the settlement, operational, and commercial risks due to delays.

In practice, the maximum time to evaluate the risks should be quicker than the maximum response time before the order is fulfilled, e.g., "pick up in under two hours" or "every fifteen minutes".

In the table below we describe the range of possible response time for automated risk evaluation and manual payment verifications.

Response time to evaluate risk
Seconds for automated screening; minutes for verifications

Type of risk evalaution	Min	Max
Automated	100ms	60s
Manual	1min	24h

14.7 Autonomous and self-learning

One last challenge of risk management solutions for e-commerce services is autonomy. Setting up and re-configuring risk man-

agement solutions periodically cost money and demand expertise.

To tackle the need for autonomy, methods from big data, artificial
intelligence (AI) and machine learning (ML) are integrated into
the risk management systems to automatically configure them.
Due to increased automation, the risk management system
gradually becomes self-learning.

In practice, the burden of re-configuring the rules and scores of
the risk management system gradually shifts from analysts, whose
work is to run ad hoc analyses to reconfigure the system, to AI and
ML algorithms, which are themselves maintained by data scientists.

This shift to AI and ML to drive the configuration of risk management systems brings an array of benefits, i.e., to *adapt faster*, to
better prevent risk, and to *require less expertise*.

Adapt faster	The risk prevention system is autonomously updated with AI; updates are done faster and more systematically at a larger scale.
Better risk prevention	Risk is prevented more pro-actively, e.g., in the case of fraud detection, a fast system update will lead to fewer repeat fraud offenders (RFOs) and hence to less payment fraud.

Less	It may be hard for independent e-commerce
expertise	services to maintain the pool of expertise
required	needed to maintain the risk prevention
	system in-house.

By adding more automation, less expertise is needed for daily management.

Repeat Fraud Offenders (RFO)
Frauds repeated with a similar modus operandi

> Fraud attempts are often repeated multiple times with a similar modus operandi; those who perpetrate such frauds are called repeat fraud offenders.

14.8 Ideal risk management: Key points

In brief

The ideal risk management system is a system that detects 100% of payment frauds, never rejects any real customers, requires no installation, demands no maintenance, responds immediately, and is autonomous and self-learning. This ideal risk management system is the north star against which we compare practical solutions.

When dealing with payment fraud, a corner case is to stop accepting payments, which is obviously impractical. Alternatively, only accepting payments when they are two-factor authenticated is a practical solution, but it is suboptimal.

In practice, validating as many true clients as possible requires trust, which can be engineered within the IT system, with fraud prevention algorithms, and with risk operation analysts carrying out manual verifications.

By relying on software as a service (SaaS) solutions, some of which need no installation, e-commerce services have low upfront investment, better reliability and performance, and no maintenance. Some of these solutions are autonomous and self-learning, which means they require less management expertise and are updated faster.

Key points

- The practically ideal risk management system *dynamically optimizes* the cost benefit of each decision at risk.

- Never rejecting a real client is possible only if there is *full trust*.

- *3D Secure* is suboptimal because it reduces checkout velocity and conversion.

- Requesting *proofs of identity and address* helps build trust but reduces checkout velocity, conversion, and buying satisfaction.

- Fraud prevention solutions in *SaaS* have low upfront cost and no maintenance; they are cost-effective and reliable.

- Some SaaS vendors require no software installations.

- Ideally, a fraud prevention solution has an immediate response time to prevent settlement, operational, and commercial risks.

- An autonomous solution requires no configuration, adapts faster, and prevents the risk of payment fraud better.

15 Risk classification, escalation time, and rating

Background The previous chapter introduced concepts of experimental design, statistical methods to carry out data analysis, and statistical learning principles to teach machines how to predict.

Problem However, what is missing is the application of these techniques to prevent the risk of payment fraud in e-commerce

169

services. This chapter and the next chapter will address these missing areas.

15.1 Classifying the different types of risks

Businesses face financial, operational, strategic, business, safety, and hazard risks [5]. The table summarizes a classification of the four types of risks and their subtypes.

Risk classification

Payment fraud is a credit risk

Risk type	#	Risk subtype
Financial	1	Pricing risk
	2	Credit risk
	3	Liquidity risk
Operational	4	Process risk
	5	IT risk
	6	Personnel risk
	7	Legal risk
Strategic and business	8	Management risk
	9	Market position risk
	10	Operating environment risk
Safety and hazard	11	Safety risk
	12	Security arrangements risk
	13	Hazard risk

Sources: [5]

Financial risks include liquidity, pricing, and credit risks. Operational risks include process, IT, personnel, and legal risks. In the rest of this section, we focus on credit and operational risks.

For e-commerce services, credit risk occurs when cardholders are victims of payment fraud or are unwilling or unable to honor payments. Hence, chargebacks for fraud reasons are one instance of credit risk.

15.2 Example of loss scenario: Credit risk

Among the different financial risks an e-commerce service faces, there is the *credit risk*, which occurs when a payment fraud materializes as a chargeback. This is what we describe in this section.

The costs associated with chargebacks include reversals of sales, chargeback fees from payment service providers, and raw material, manufacturing, and shipping costs. In the following table, we report a breakdown for merchants that resell or manufacture products.

Credit risk in e-commerce services
Chargebacks cost more than the sale's value

		Resellers			Manufacturers	
	Gross margin	5%	15%	30%	60%	90%
Sales	Value	100				
Charge-back	Reversal	-100				
	Fee (PSP)	-15				
PSP	Fee	-3				
Costs	Raw material	-95	-85	-70	-40	-10
	Manufacturing	N/A			-30	-60
	Shipping		-5	-10	-15	-20
	Total	-113	-108	-98	-103	-108

Sources: simulation of a cost breakdown after a chargeback has occurred

15.3 Example of loss scenario: Settlement risk

Previously, we described the financial consequences of charge-backs, which is an instance of *credit risk*. Now, we describe an instance of *settlement risk* that exists from the moment the payment is acquired till the moment the product packages are delivered by the shipping carrier.

Once an e-commerce service has received a payment, it fills the order. If the ordered products are not digital, the merchant ships the product with one or more carriers. Most of the time, deliveries are successfully completed.

However, they may not be completed in some instances, e.g., if the package never arrives or if it arrives but is damaged. These situations are examples of a settlement risk because the buyer is still expecting to receive the counterparty of its payment.

Similar to the previous table, in the following table we provide a breakdown of the costs associated with a shipment that never arrives. Compared to chargebacks, which are a credit risk, a settlement risk is an operational risk. Note that the financial risk is lower than that for chargebacks.

Settlement risk in e-commerce services
Shipments that do not arrive are an important risk

	Gross margin	Resellers			Manufacturers	
		5%	15%	30%	60%	90%
Sales	Value			100		
PSP	Fee			-3		
Ship #1	Raw material	-95	-85	-70	-40	-10
	Manufacturing		N/A		-30	-60
	Shipping		-5	-10	-15	-20
Ship #2	Raw material	-95	-85	-70	-40	-10
	Manufacturing		N/A		-30	-60
	Shipping		-5	-10	-15	-20
	Total	-93	-83	-63	-73	-83

Sources: simulation of a cost breakdown for shipment that never arrive

15.4 Example of loss scenario: Operational risk

Previous two sections describe the financial consequences associated with chargebacks (*credit risk*) and non-arrived shipments (*settlement risk*). Now, we analyze the financial consequences of a *faulty product* on an e-commerce service.

In the table below, we provide a breakdown of the cost in the event that:

1. the product does not match the quality defined by the merchant;

2. the quality expected by the buyer; or

3. the quality required by legal regulations.

As expected, this risk is lower than those for chargebacks or shipments that do not arrive.

Faulty product risk in e-commerce services
Cash-neutral for resellers; one more risk for manufacturers

	Gross margin	Resellers			Manufacturers	
		5%	15%	30%	60%	90%
Sales	Value	100				
PSP	Fee	-3				
Ship #1	Raw material	-95	-85	-70	-40	-10
	Manufacturing		N/A		-30	-60
	Shipping			-5	-10	-15 / -20
Replaced product	Raw material		N/A		N/A	
	Manufacturing		N/A		-30	-60
	Shipping			-5	-10	-15 / -20
	Total	2	2	7	-13	-23

Sources: simulation of the breakdown of costs when products are faulty; resellers transfer the liability of the loss to manufacturers

15.5 Escalation time: Defining the concept

Previous sections introduced a classification of the different risks and their risk subtypes. Then, we reviewed three loss scenarios for e-commerce services in the case of chargebacks (*credit risk*), non-arrived shipments (*settlement risk*), and faulty products.

Here, we lay the foundation for the concept of the *escalation time* of a fraud. In the context of e-commerce services, the escalation time defines as follows.

Escalation time
Delay between payment acquisition and fraud notification

> It is the time between when a payment is acquired and when it is reported by the acquirer as a payment fraud.

Having a precise understanding of the escalation time is important when making credit risk calculations, because fraud risk depends on the time between the payment acquisition and the time the risk is evaluated. The longer the time range, the less likely it is that a payment fraud may occur on a payment.

For instance, if we assume the risk of payment fraud to be 0.8%, we know that four weeks after a payment was made the risk will halved (0.4%) and that after six months, there won't be any more credit risk because all the chargebacks will have been escalated by then.

A variety of reasons explain why escalation time exists. The primary delay is due to the time the cardholder or issuing bank needs to discover the payment fraud. Once it is discovered, there are at least three possible pathways to escalate a notification of fraud: *complete escalation, from issuer to acquirer*, and via *law enforcement*.

Complete escalation   Once the payment fraud has been discovered by the issuing side, one escalation path is to notify the card schemes, which notifies the acquirer, which itself notifies the merchant.

From issuer to acquirer   Alternatively, the issuer may reach the acquirer or merchant directly, e.g., if they are in the same domestic market.

Law enforcement   Law enforcement agencies may notify the merchant when the chargeback has been declared to them.

15.6 Escalation time: Empirical distribution

In previous section we introduced the concept of *escalation time*. Now, we illustrate it with actual data, which we refer to as the escalation time's empirical distribution.

It is possible to estimate the e-commerce service's and acquirer's typical escalation times by collecting historical dates of chargebacks. The following figure illustrates a sample distribution of escalation time for an ubivar.com client.

Escalation time's empirical distribution
More than 30 days on average to escalate a payment fraud

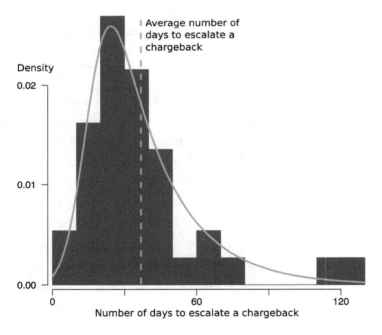

Sources: ubivar.com client

We find that 50% of chargebacks are escalated within 3 to 5 weeks and 90% to 95% are escalated within 3 months but, in some instances, chargebacks can take as long as six months to escalate.

15.7 Escalation time: Estimating the model

In the following table, we summarize the parameters of an exponentially modified gaussian distribution estimated on the sample distribution of the escalation time [86].

Escalation time model estimates
30 days on average to escalate a payment fraud

	Estimate	Standard error
μ	15.3	3.3
σ	7.6	2.4
λ	4.6×10^{-2}	1.0×10^{-2}
$\mu + \frac{1}{\lambda}$	36.9	(mean)

Sources: Ubivar.com client ($n = 37$)

The exponentially modified Gaussian has the following probability density function [86]:

$$p_{et}(t) = \frac{\lambda}{2} e^{\frac{\lambda}{2}(2\mu + \lambda\sigma^2 - 2t)} erfc\left(\frac{\mu + \lambda\sigma^2 - t}{\sqrt{2}\sigma}\right) \qquad (15.1)$$

where μ is the mean of the normal distribution, σ is the standard deviation of the normal distribution, and λ is the rate of the exponential.

Then, the probability $P(E|\delta t, Y)$ that a payment fraud Y is still to be escalated E a period of δt days after the payment acquisition is the complementary of the cumulative distribution function:

$$P(E|\delta t, Y) = 1 - \int_0^t p_{et}(t)dt \qquad (15.2)$$

The minimum and maximum values of $P(E|\delta t, Y)$ are attained:

- $\delta t = 0$, then $P(E|\delta t, Y) = 1$
- $\delta t \to \infty$, then $P(E|\delta t, Y) = 0$

In practice, when $\delta t >> 121$ (4 months), then $P(E|\delta t, Y) \to 1$.

Finally, an upper bound at the α-level for $P(E|\delta t, Y)$ can be estimated using the confidence interval relation of a binomial proportion [59]:

$$CI_\alpha[P(E|\delta t, Y)] = P(E|\delta t, Y) + z_\alpha \sqrt{\frac{P(E|\delta t, Y)(1 - P(E|\delta t, Y))}{n_Y}}$$

$$(15.3)$$

with α the significance level of the confidence interval (CI); the multiplier $z_{\frac{\alpha}{2}}$, which comes from the normal curve and determines the significance level; and n_Y, the sample size for the model fit [59].

15.8 Ratings for payments and portfolios

Similar to Standard & Poor's [42], Moody's [28], and other credit rating agencies, it is possible to rate the credit risk [74] (payment fraud) of commands made on e-commerce services.

It is also possible to give a rating to a portfolio composed of orders, which have individual risks of payment fraud.

In contrast to the value at risk (VAR) estimates (we will dive into VAR in the next chapter), which converts probabilities back to the currency value, credit ratings map the credit risk of orders ($P(Y|\delta t, X_i)$) and portfolios ($\Sigma_i P(Y|\delta t, X_i)$) to an ordinal classification at a given time horizon, e.g., 1 month or 1 year.

A simplified example of credit rating is given in the table below.

Credit risk ratings
Ba and B for highest risks; Aaa, Aa, A for lowest risks

	Default rate horizon	
	1 Month	1 Year
Aaa	0.00%	0.00%
Aa	0.10%	0.20%
A	0.20%	0.40%
Baa	0.40%	0.80%
Ba	0.80%	1.60%
B	1.60%	3.20%

15.9 Risk classification, escalation and ratings: Key points

In brief

Risk can be classified into financial, operational, strategic and business, and safety and hazards risks. A payment fraud event is a type of credit risk; after the reversal, chargebacks cost more than the sale's value. A non-arrived shipment is a type of settlement risk; this risk is nearly as important as that of chargebacks. A faulty product is a type of operational risk, but the merchant is not liable.

There are at least three instances of escalation paths for payment fraud: a complete escalation (from cardholder to issuer, card scheme, acquirer, and merchant), a direct escalation (from issuer to acquirer), and an escalation from a law enforcement agency to the merchant. Each path has its own escalation time. It is possible to model the escalation time.

Finally, it is possible to rate individual payments and sets of payments for their credit risk (payment fraud). This approach is related to what Standard and Poor's and Moody's do when they rate the debts of countries and companies.

Key points

- Payment fraud is a *financial/credit risk*.

- A non-arrived shipment is an *operational/settlement risk*.

- Payment fraud and non-arrived shipments are a very significant risk in e-commerce services.

- The escalation time is the number of days elapsed between the payment acquisition and the notification of fraud.

- On average, it takes three to five weeks to escalate a payment fraud.

- Almost all payment frauds are escalated after four to six months.

- Payment frauds are escalated to merchants by various channels, such as law enforcement, issuers, or card networks.

- Ratings are an instrument to grade the credit risk of a transaction or of a portfolio.

16   Piloting risk in e-commerce services with value at risk

Background   We presented a typical fraud prevention process, detailed its internal components, laid out the necessary foundations for data analysis to be carried out, and introduced elements of experimental design, statistics, and statistical learning.

Statistical learning models could sit on top of this very complex data analysis process, and data scientists could manage these models. However, we would miss the opportunity to bridge the gap between machine language and our usual decision-making framework based on *financial costs*.

16 Piloting risk in e-commerce services with value at risk

Problem   Previously, we mentioned that the ideal risk management system dynamically optimizes the cost benefit of each decision at risk. In this chapter, we will review how this is possible with the help of value at risk (VAR).

16.1 VAR: Its origin, principle, and advantages

VAR is a financial concept attributed to Tim Guldimann, who developed it in the late 1980s, when he was head of global research at JP Morgan [23].

It is a method used to evaluate losses that won't be exceeded over a target time horizon and with a given significance level. Target horizons may be days, weeks, months, quarters, or years, and significance levels could be 5%, 1%, or 0.1% [23, 129].

When measuring risk, an advantage of VAR is that it uses the same units as those used by companies to pilot their activity and monitor their bottom-line, i.e., dollars, euros, pounds, etc. These units are widely understood. In the opposite, credit ratings (e.g., Aaa, B) or percent values of risks (e.g., 1.2%, 0.2%) are only understood by professionals involved in risk management and finance.

Another advantage is that VAR can be used to aggregate the total risk of a portfolio of transactions, which is very convenient when evaluating a business' exposure to risk, to budgeting the risk, and managing a portfolio.

16.2 VAR of one payment

The likelihood for an order i to be a fraudulent payment over a time horizon δt is:

$$P(Y|\delta t, X_i) = P(Y|X_i) \times P(E|\delta t, Y) \qquad (16.1)$$

where $P(Y|X_i)$ is the risk score of the payment, X_i is a vector of the financial variables, and $P(E|\delta t, Y)$ is the likelihood that a fraudulent payment is *still* to be escalated δt days after the order has been made.

In order to describe the degree of uncertainty that we have and considering $P(E|\delta t, Y)$ as a fixed population parameter[1], then an upper confidence bound at the α-level for $P(Y|\delta t, X_i)$ can be estimated using the confidence interval relation of a binomial proportion:

$$CI_\alpha[P(Y|\delta t, X_i)] = P(Y|\delta t, X_i) + z_{\frac{\alpha}{2}} \sqrt{\frac{P(Y|\delta t, X_i)(1 - P(Y|\delta t, X_i))}{n}}$$
$$(16.2)$$

where n is the data set size used to estimate the risk score $P(Y|Xi)$, α is the significance level, and z is the multiplier from the normal curve which determines the significance level.

We then calculate the expected value at risk (VAR) of a sale i as:

$$\text{VAR}_i = P(Y|\delta t, X_i) \times V_i \qquad (16.3)$$

An upper bound of VAR_i at a significance level α is estimated by:

$$CI_\alpha[\text{VAR}_i] = CI_\alpha[P(Y|\delta t, X_i)] \times V_i. \qquad (16.4)$$

---

[1]This parameter is estimated from the history of chargebacks, *prior* to the modeling of $P(Y|\delta t, X_i)$.

If the value at risk (VAR$_i$) is subtracted from the sale's value (V_i), we have a sale's *real* value with the average cost of the risk integrated (see figure below for an illustration):

$$V_i^R = V_i - \text{VAR}_i \tag{16.5}$$
$$= (1 - P(Y|\delta t, X_i)) \times V_i \tag{16.6}$$

Sale's value with risk subtracted

The average cost of the risk is integrated into the sale's price

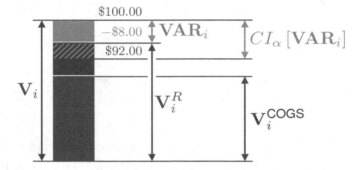

Following these notations, the amount of funds left after deducting the costs of goods sold (COGS) from a sale's value is given by:

$$V_i^{\text{COGS}} = F_i(COGS) \times V_i, \tag{16.7}$$

with $F_i(COGS)$ the gross margin.

Finally, we can build a decision function that determines the most appropriate treatment for transaction i. The different cases are reported in the following table.

Based on the company's strategy, the risk management service will estimate a threshold δ^R from the empirical distribution of

VAR-based arbitrage function

The merchant sees a loss when the risk exceeds the margin

VAR_i	V_i^R	$V_i^R - V_i^{COGS}$	#	Risk; expected gain
$= 0$	$= V_i$	$= V_i^{COGS}$	1	None, 0%; sale's margin
$< V_i - V_i^{COGS}$	$> V_i^{COGS}$	> 0	2	Tolerated (α); positive
$= V_i - V_i^{COGS}$	$= V_i^{COGS}$	$= 0$	3	Breakeven; zero
$= V_i$	$= 0$	$= -V_i^{COGS}$	4	Full, 100%; loose COGS

risk scores in order to specify the *percent amount* of payments to verify. Thereby stabilizing the number of reviews per reviewer and per day, which has a direct implication on the reduction of operational cost and efficiency.

Then, the decision function would be:

$$\text{if sgn}\left(V_i^R - V_i^{COGS} - \delta^R\right) = \begin{cases} < 0, & \text{then review} \\ \geq 0, & \text{otherwise accept.} \end{cases} \quad (16.8)$$

16.3 VAR of all payments

As mentioned earlier in this chapter, VAR is a method that can aggregate the risk of individual transactions into a value at risk.

Therefore, the total expected VAR is estimated as follows:

$$\text{VAR} = \Sigma_{i=1}^n P(Y|\delta t, X_i) \times V_i, \quad (16.9)$$

where $P(Y|\delta t, X_i)$ is the likelihood of a payment to be a payment fraud, δt is the number of days after a payment has been acquired or executed, X_i is a vector of financial variables, V_i is the sale's value, and n is the number of orders in the portfolio.

Given the total VAR, it is possible to estimate the proportion of the total sales that is at risk:

$$P_{\text{VAR}} = \frac{\text{VAR}}{\Sigma_i^n V_i}. \tag{16.10}$$

An upper bound at the α-level for P_{VAR} can be estimated using the confidence interval relation of a binomial proportion:

$$CI_\alpha[P_{\text{VAR}}] = P_{\text{VAR}} + z_{\frac{\alpha}{2}} \sqrt{\frac{P_{\text{VAR}}(1 - P_{\text{VAR}})}{n}} \tag{16.11}$$

where n is the significance level and $z_{\frac{\alpha}{2}}$ is the multiplier from the normal curve for that significance level. Finally, an upper bound of the total expected VAR is expressed as follows:

$$CI_\alpha[\text{VAR}] = CI_\alpha[P_{\text{VAR}}] \times \Sigma_i^n V_i. \tag{16.12}$$

Total exposure to risk
Adding the average cost of the risk for all sales

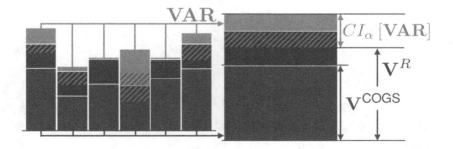

16.4 VAR: Some limitations

Two limitations of VAR are its reliance on the *independence assumption* and the *underestimation of extreme values*.

Independence assumption

In practice, orders made on e-commerce service are not independent of each other.

First, real buyers are likely to make repeated purchases on e-commerce services, especially if some sort of subscription has been set up (e.g., Amazon Prime).

Second, if fraudsters identify weaknesses in an e-commerce service, they are likely to commit repeat fraud offenses (RFOs).

This means that the financial variables, X_i, are not independent, which may lead to overestimates or underestimates of the VAR and confidence intervals.

Underestimated extreme values

The normal distribution may not be the most appropriate distribution to estimate the confidence interval of VAR.

One way to control this is to take into consideration the autocorrelation of the identified frauds to improve our VAR prediction.

Indeed, extreme events such as those that model credit risk may occur more frequently than what the normal distribution would estimate.

To tackle the fat tail problem, methods from extreme value theory exists [91].

16.5 Piloting risk with VAR: Key points

In brief

One issue with sum scores, risk scores, and ratings is that they are not in a unit, which everyone understand in a business. Instead, value at risk (VAR) is expressed in terms of notional amounts, which enables the firm to make comparable and standardized decisions.

Another advantage of VAR is that it is estimated per payment and it can be aggregated per portfolio, thereby providing a total estimate of a business's risk.

In addition, because VAR derives from traditional statistical methods, it is very easy to adapt the risk level tolerated by the business and the likelihood that the risk materializes, i.e., the significance level.

However, one limitation of VAR is that it assumes independence, which may not hold because real clients may repeat purchases and fraudsters may repeat fraud attempts, thereby introducing correlation between purchases.

Another limitation is that the normal distribution may underestimate the likelihood of extreme values, which is known as the fat tail of a distribution.

Key points

- VAR aims to estimate the worst possible loss at a given time horizon (e.g., one month) and significance level (e.g., 1%).

- VAR derives from traditional statistical methods; it is easy to adapt the VAR parameters to the specific needs of the business.

- VAR can aggregate the risk of individual transactions into a total VAR.

- VAR assumes independence between risk events, which does not hold in practice.

- VAR may underestimate the frequency of rare events because it is based on the normal distribution.

Concluding remarks

Risk management intelligence: Final walk through

Choices related to online payment processing tend to change slowly. Notably, several payment methods that existed before the internet, such as checks and payment cards, remain, along with other methods that only exist online, such as direct banking and PayPal.

With such a diverse landscape of payment methods, payment processing intermediaries exist to help settle payments online. Payment intermediaries have specific roles and rules that are often defined by card schemes. They help establish the necessary trust for online payments.

Concluding remarks

When payment intermediaries fail to guarantee this trust, payment fraud and chargebacks happen, which is a type of credit risk. The driving force for fraud is the act of reselling credit card numbers obtained cheaply via hacking, phishing, or social engineering , on the black market.

Depending on their margins, e-commerce services are tolerant or intolerant to fraud, and their risk levels are low, medium, or high depending on their international exposure and product catalogs. They may need to manage payment fraud; if so, they use fraud detection systems and/or 3D Secure.

In-house, legacy, and dedicated fraud prevention systems exist. Frequently, they are composed of black-, gray-, and whitelists; rules that are based on thresholds or matching; and risk scores. These scores are either calibrated manually or automatically by optimization algorithms. If these systems suspect payment fraud, they may automatically reject the payment or send it for verification.

If the payment is sent for verification, risk operation analysts review the payment characteristics. They may validate the payment or reject it if they believe it bears too much risk. If doubt persists, they may also request an internal or external peer review.

Once the payment is validated, e-commerce services proceed to delivery. If the shipping carrier fails to deliver the products, the merchant faces a settlement risk because it received the payment counterparty but failed to fulfill its promise to ship the product.

The escalation time is the time between a payment acquisition and a fraud notification. It takes three to five weeks to escalate 50% of all fraud cases and three to four months to escalate 90% of those cases. Once a fraud case is reported, the system is updated to prevent future fraud cases with the same modus operandi.

The configuration of fraud detection systems may be done by e-commerce services, experts, or vendors of fraud detection solutions. The techniques used to parameterize these systems are based on statistics, machine learning, and financial risk management.

Risk management intelligence software helps parameterize fraud detection systems, carry out payment verifications, and audit the fraud management process. They help prevent payment fraud by returning fewer false positives and false negatives. They also help speed up the risk management process.

Pathways to improve how risk is managed

There are at least four possible pathways to improving how credit card fraud is prevented in e-commerce services: *designing better algorithms, adding data of better quality, improving the design of IT systems*, and *raising the average level of expertise*.

Designing better algorithms   The first pathway is to design more accurate algorithms to detect fraud.

One way is to update parameters for rules and scores as fast as possible when new cases of fraud are detected.

Another way is to create algorithms that can consider the cost of each type of error, i.e., failing to detect fraud or suggesting that a payment is fraud when it is a payment from a real client.

Adding data of better quality

The second path is to improve the quantity and quality of data used by fraud detection systems.

The poor design of the current information systems limits how data is used, particularly to audit risks and predict the likelihood of fraud.

In addition, many e-merchants lack data, which makes them more vulnerable to risk, e.g., when entering new markets or when accepting more types of payment methods.

Designing better IT systems

The third pathway is to improve the design of information systems used to verify payments.

Here, the aim is to not only automate most of the recurring tasks e.g., preparing audit reports or updating lists, but also reduce the number of applications analysts use when verifying payments (typically, analysts switch between reservation system(s), Google, social media accounts, email software, and various other websites).

Raising expertise level   The fourth path is to raise the average level of expertise in managing payment fraud.

This can be done by having analysts pass the Certified Fraud Examiners (CFE) exam [31] and by offering other forms of training, e.g., webinars, white papers, online articles, and conferences, targeting e-commerce analysts and decisions makers.

Our vision: Nine points

Here, we share part of our vision of fraud detection and risk management intelligence. There are nine points, which relate to *tech*nical evolution, general *trends*, and *risk* management.

Risk in e-commerce services: The future

Autonomy, speed, and scale with more data, SaaS, accuracy

Type	#	Vision
Tech	1	Blacklist and risk scores should adapt autonomously.
	2	Numerically optimized risk scores should replace sum scores, because of their better calibration.
	3	Whitelists will remain, because they help filter payments and are setup only once, but scoring rules and lists should be deprecated because they are badly calibrated, and their effectiveness drifts over time.
	4	Value at risk (VAR) will generalize to more small and medium businesses (SMB) because it is simple to understand and it helps everyone value the risk at a transaction- and a business-level.
Trends	5	Workers shift from data production (configuring or making audit reports), to data consumption.
	6	Specialized vendors should manage fraud prevention to allow data-pooling and help with legal compliance.
	7	As data transfers accelerate between payment intermediaries, fraud escalation time will reduce, thereby reducing the number of repeat fraud offenses.
	8	Hacking, phishing, and social engineering increase in technicality, speed, and volume, thereby stressing the need for risk management intelligence.
Risk	9	Risk management intelligence will help e-commerce services adapt faster, reduce risk exposure, boost conversion, and reduce the burden of managing risks.

Where to go from here

You've read through this book and checked out the resources on my blog (`fabricecolas.me`), and now you'd like to implement some of these ideas at your company.

– What next? What steps can you take?

This is what we will see in the next sections.

Companies and institutions to follow

In the table below are listed several companies and institutions that we follow because of the high quality of the information or reporting that they produce, or the services that they offer.

Online information and services
Service providers; regulatory bodies; and report providers

Risk and fraud	Merchant risk council
	`merchantriskcouncil.org`
	Web based fraud prevention community
	`perseuss.com`

Data protection	European data protection supervisor
	`edps.europa.eu`
	French data protection authority (CNIL)
	`cnil.fr`

Reports	News and statistics for card and mobile payment
	`nilsonreport.com`
	Obervatory for payment card security from the
	Banque de France
	`observatoire.banque-france.fr/en/`

Contact us and/or check out our site for additional free resources

We can help you with on-site training in France and abroad. We provide expert advice regarding your business' systems or management of risk. We have software that is available as a service. And we provide support in risk management intelligence.

 rmi@fabricecolas.me

+33 9 87 67 52 52

Index

Bibliography

[1] AriadNEXT. 2d-doc. http://www.2d-doc.com/, 2017.

[2] A. Aschengrau and G.R. Seage. *Essentials of Epidemiology in Public Health*. Jones & Bartlett Learning, 2014.

[3] J. D. Banfield and A. E. Raftery. Model-based gaussian and non-gaussian clustering. *Biometrics*, 49:803–821, 1993.

[4] Bigcommerce. What are the interchange fees and how are they calculated? https://www.bigcommerce.com/ecommerce-answers/what-are-interchange-fees-and-how-are-they-calculated/, 2017.

[5] Cargotec. Risk classification. http://www.cargotec.com/en-global/investors/Governance/Internal-control-and-risk-management/Pages/Risk-classification.aspx, 2017.

[6] CNN. Target settles for $39 million over data breach. http://money.cnn.com/2015/12/02/news/companies/target-data-breach-settlement/, December 2015.

[7] Nello Cristianini and John Shawe-Taylor. *An Introduction to Support Vector Machines: And Other Kernel-based Learning Methods*. Cambridge University Press, New York, NY, USA, 2000.

[8] Banque de France. Observatoire de la sécurité des cartes bancaires. https://observatoire.banque-france.fr/uploads/media/OSCP-rapport-annuel-2015.pdf, 2015.

[9] A. P. Dempster, N. M. Laird, and D. B. Rubin. Maximum likelihood from incomplete data via the em algorithm. *Journal of the royal statistical society, series b*, 39(1):1–38, 1977.

[10] Brian Everitt. *Cluster analysis*. Heinemann Educational Books Ltd, 1974.

[11] American Express. American express interchange fees. https://www.americanexpress.com/us/content/merchant/streamline-payments/payment-solutions.html, 2017.

[12] Fee.org. Why pay for things, fee.org. https://fee.org/articles/why-pay-for-things/, 2017.

[13] Forbes. Discover financial services. http://www.forbes.com/companies/discover-financial-services/, 2017.

[14] George Forman. An extensive empirical study of feature selection metrics for text classification. *J. Mach. Learn. Res.*, 3:1289–1305, March 2003.

[15] Johannes Fürnkranz. Pairwise classification as an ensemble technique. In T. Elomaa, Heikki Mannila, and Hannu Toivonen, editors, *Proceedings of the 13th European Conference on Machine Learning (ECML-02)*, volume 2430 of *Lecture Notes in Artificial Intelligence*, pages 97–110, Helsinki, Finland, 2002. Springer-Verlag.

[16] Geek. Verizon is shutting down netflix competitor redbox instant. http://www.geek.com/mobile/verizon-is-shutting-down-netflix-competitor-redbox-instant-1606244/, August 2014.

[17] A.N. Glaser. *High-yield Biostatistics*. High-yield series. Lippincott Williams & Wilkins, 2001.

[18] Joseph Grifone. *Algèbre Linéaire*. Cépaduès-Éditions, 1994.

[19] Isabelle Guyon and André Elisseeff. An introduction to variable and feature selection. http://www.jmlr.org/papers/volume3/guyon03a/guyon03a.pdf, 2003.

[20] Trevor Hastie, Robert Tibshirani, and Jerome Friedman. *The Elements of Statistical Learning*. Springer Series in Statistics. Springer New York Inc., New York, NY, USA, 2001.

[21] Indiatimes.com. Sbi becomes top merchant acquiring bank in country. http://timesofindia.indiatimes.com/business/india-business/SBI-becomes-top-merchant-acquiring-bank-in-country/articleshow/52505867.cms, 2017.

[22] Informationisbeautiful.net. Major data breaches. http://www.informationisbeautiful.net/visualizations/worlds-biggest-data-breaches-hacks/, 2017.

[23] Philippe Jorion. Value at risk, the new benchmark for managing financial risk.

[24] Kapronasia. Unique acquirer ranking published by chinese payments association. https://www.kapronasia.com/china-payments-research-category/item/759-unique-acquirer-ranking-published-by-chinese-payments-association.html, 2017.

[25] Ron Kohavi and George H. John. Wrappers for feature subset selection, artificial intelligence, 1997. https://pdfs.semanticscholar.org/0048/88621a4e4cee56b6633338a89aa036cf5ae5.pdf, May 1996.

[26] MasterCard. Mastercard interchange fees. https://www.mastercard.us/en-us/about-mastercard/what-we-do/interchange.html, 2017.

[27] Thomas M. Mitchell. *Machine Learning*. McGraw-Hill, Inc., New York, NY, USA, 1 edition, 1997.

[28] Moody's. Website. https://www.moodys.com/, 2017.

[29] Mycardpaymentblog. Top credit card issuers in india, mycardpaymentblog. https://mycardpaymentblog.wordpress.com/2016/05/30/2015-top-credit-card-issuers-in-india-comparison-of-last-4-years/, May 2016.

[30] Nasdaq. Cpi. `http://www.nasdaq.com/markets/ipos/company/cpi-card-group-inc-972592-79140`, 2017.

[31] Association of Certified Fraud Examiners. Website. `http://www.acfe.com/`, 2017.

[32] Krebs on Security. Banks: Credit card breach at home depot. `http://krebsonsecurity.com/2014/09/banks-credit-card-breach-at-home-depot/`, September 2014.

[33] The Huffington Post. Target hacked: Retailer confirms 'unauthorized access' of credit card data. `http://www.huffingtonpost.com/2013/12/19/target-hacked-customer-credit-card-data-accessed_n_4471672.html?utm_hp_ref=mostpopular`), Decembre 2013.

[34] Nilson report. Issue 1071. (`https://cdn2.hubspot.net/hubfs/1676180/Resources/Nilson_Report__1071.pdf?t=1468422071303`, November 2015.

[35] Nilson report. Issue 1082. `https://electronicpayments.com/assets/media-docs/Nilson-Report-1082.pdf`, March 2016.

[36] Nilson report. Issue 1087. `https://www.featurespace.co.uk/wp-content/uploads/Nilson-Report-May-16-part-2.pdf`, May 2016.

[37] Nilson report. Issue 1999. `http://files.constantcontact.com/610724ae101/c234992b-e060-4cba-884a-8949c9d1198e.pdf`, November 2016.

[38] Nilson Report. Nilson report. `https://www.nilsonreport.com`, 2017.

[39] Reuters. Jpmorgan hack exposed data of 83 million, among biggest breaches in history. `http://www.reuters.com/article/us-jpmorgan-cybersecurity-idUSKCN0HR23T20141003`, October 2014.

[40] MasterCard Payment Gateway Services. 3d secure. `http://www.mastercard.com/gateway/implementation_guides/3D-Secure.html`, 2017.

[41] Tobias Sing, Oliver Sander, Niko Beerenwinkel, and Thomas Lengauer. Visualizing the performance of scoring classifiers, rocr r package. `https://rocr.bioinf.mpi-sb.mpg.de/ROCR.pdf`, May 2013.

[42] Standard and Poor's. Website. `https://www.standardandpoors.com`, 2017.

[43] Statista. Number of credit cards in circulation worldwide. `https://www.statista.com/statistics/279257/number-of-credit-cards-in-circulation-worldwide/`, 2017.

[44] Statista. Number of paypal's total active registered user accounts from 1st quarter 2010 to 4th quarter 2016 (in millions). `https://www.statista.com/statistics/218493/paypals-total-active-registered-accounts-from-2010/`, 2017.

[45] TechCrunch. Weebly hacked, 43 million credentials stolen. `https://techcrunch.com/2016/10/20/weebly-hacked-43-million-credentials-stolen/`, October 2016.

[46] New York Times. Jpmorgan chase hacking affects 76 million households. `https://dealbook.nytimes.com/2014/10/02/jpmorgan-discovers-further-cyber-security-issues/?_php=true&_type=blogs&_r=1`, October 2014.

[47] The Verge. Redbox instant streaming video service shutting down on october 7th. `http://www.theverge.com/2014/10/4/6908181/redbox-instant-streaming-video-service-shutting-down-on-october-7th`, October 2014.

[48] Vérifiance. Chiffres clés, vérifiance. `https://www.verifiance-fnci.fr`, 2017.

[49] Wikipedia. 3-d secure, — Wikipedia, the free encyclopedia. `https://en.wikipedia.org/wiki/3-D_Secure`, 2017.

[50] Wikipedia. A/b testing, — Wikipedia, the free encyclopedia. `https://en.wikipedia.org/wiki/A/B_testing`, 2017.

[51] Wikipedia. Akaike information criterion, — Wikipedia, the free encyclopedia. https://en.wikipedia.org/wiki/Akaike_information_criterion, 2017.

[52] Wikipedia. Algorithm, — Wikipedia, the free encyclopedia. https://en.wikipedia.org/wiki/Algorithm, 2017.

[53] Wikipedia. Algorithm, wiktionary. https://en.wiktionary.org/wiki/algorithm, 2017.

[54] Wikipedia. American express, — Wikipedia, the free encyclopedia. https://en.wikipedia.org/wiki/American_Express, 2017.

[55] Wikipedia. Application programming interface, — Wikipedia, the free encyclopedia. https://en.wikipedia.org/wiki/Application_programming_interface, 2017.

[56] Wikipedia. Automated clearing house, — Wikipedia, the free encyclopedia. https://en.wikipedia.org/wiki/Automated_Clearing_House, 2017.

[57] Wikipedia. Bancomat, — Wikipedia, the free encyclopedia. https://en.wikipedia.org/wiki/Bancomat_(debit_card), 2017.

[58] Wikipedia. Bayesian information criterion, — Wikipedia, the free encyclopedia. https://en.wikipedia.org/wiki/Bayesian_information_criterion, 2017.

[59] Wikipedia. Binomial proportion confidence interval, — Wikipedia, the free encyclopedia. https://en.wikipedia.org/wiki/Binomial_proportion_confidence_interval, 2017.

[60] Wikipedia. Bitcoin, — Wikipedia, the free encyclopedia. https://en.wikipedia.org/wiki/Bitcoin, 2017.

[61] Wikipedia. Card scheme, — Wikipedia, the free encyclopedia. https://en.wikipedia.org/wiki/Card_scheme, 2017.

[62] Wikipedia. Carte bleue, — Wikipedia, the free encyclopedia. https://en.wikipedia.org/wiki/Carte_Bleue, 2017.

[63] Wikipedia. Categorical variable, — Wikipedia, the free encyclopedia. https://en.wikipedia.org/wiki/Categorical_variable, 2017.

[64] Wikipedia. Chapter 4: Types of fraud and loss, wepay. https://www.wepay.com/api/payments-101/payments-fraud-and-loss, 2017.

[65] Wikipedia. Chi-square test, — Wikipedia, the free encyclopedia. https://en.wikipedia.org/wiki/Chi-squared_test, 2017.

[66] Wikipedia. China, unionpay — Wikipedia, the free encyclopedia. https://en.wikipedia.org/wiki/China_UnionPay, 2017.

[67] Wikipedia. Coinbase, — Wikipedia, the free encyclopedia. (https://en.wikipedia.org/wiki/Coinbase), 2017.

[68] Wikipedia. Coinify, — Wikipedia, the free encyclopedia. https://en.wikipedia.org/wiki/Coinify, 2017.

[69] Wikipedia. Coinkite, — Wikipedia, the free encyclopedia. https://en.wikipedia.org/wiki/Coinkite, 2017.

[70] Wikipedia. Confidence intervals, — Wikipedia, the free encyclopedia. https://en.wikipedia.org/wiki/Confidence_interval, 2017.

[71] Wikipedia. Contingency table, — Wikipedia, the free encyclopedia. https://en.wikipedia.org/wiki/Contingency_table, 2017.

[72] Wikipedia. Continuous and discrete variables, — Wikipedia, the free encyclopedia. https://en.wikipedia.org/wiki/Continuous_and_discrete_variables, 2017.

[73] Wikipedia. Coupon, — Wikipedia, the free encyclopedia. https://en.wikipedia.org/wiki/Coupon, 2017.

[74] Wikipedia. Credit rating, — Wikipedia, the free encyclopedia. https://en.wikipedia.org/wiki/Credit_rating, 2017.

[75] Wikipedia. Customer lifetime value, — Wikipedia, the free encyclopedia. https://en.wikipedia.org/wiki/Customer_lifetime_value, 2017.

[76] Wikipedia. Data points, — Wikipedia, the free encyclopedia. https://en.wikipedia.org/wiki/Data_point, 2017.

[77] Wikipedia. Data reduction, — Wikipedia, the free encyclopedia. https://en.wikipedia.org/wiki/Data_reduction, 2017.

[78] Wikipedia. Data set, — Wikipedia, the free encyclopedia. https://en.wikipedia.org/wiki/Data_set, 2017.

[79] Wikipedia. Data transformation, — Wikipedia, the free encyclopedia. https://en.wikipedia.org/wiki/Data_transformation_(statistics), 2017.

[80] Wikipedia. Deep learning, — Wikipedia, the free encyclopedia. https://en.wikipedia.org/wiki/Deep_learning, 2017.

[81] Wikipedia. Dependent and independent variables. https://en.wikipedia.org/wiki/Dependent_and_independent_variables, 2017.

[82] Wikipedia. Dimension, — Wikipedia, the free encyclopedia. https://en.wikipedia.org/wiki/Dimension, 2017.

[83] Wikipedia. Dimensionality reduction, — Wikipedia, the free encyclopedia. https://en.wikipedia.org/wiki/Dimensionality_reduction, 2017.

[84] Wikipedia. Diners club international, — Wikipedia, the free encyclopedia. https://en.wikipedia.org/wiki/Diners_Club_International, 2017.

[85] Wikipedia. Discover card, — Wikipedia, the free encyclopedia. https://en.wikipedia.org/wiki/Discover_Card, 2017.

[86] Wikipedia. Exponentially modified gaussian distribution, — Wikipedia, the free encyclopedia. https://en.wikipedia.org/wiki/Exponentially_modified_Gaussian_distribution, 2017.

[87] Wikipedia. Fisher's exact test, — Wikipedia, the free encyclopedia. `https://en.wikipedia.org/wiki/Fisher's_exact_test`, 2017.

[88] Wikipedia. Fncpi, fichier national des chèques irréguliers, — Wikipedia, the free encyclopedia. `https://fr.wikipedia.org/wiki/Fichier_national_des_ch%C3%A8ques_irr%C3%A9guliers`, 2017.

[89] Wikipedia. Gemalto, — Wikipedia, the free encyclopedia. `https://en.wikipedia.org/wiki/Gemalto`, 2017.

[90] Wikipedia. Gene knockout, — Wikipedia, the free encyclopedia. `https://en.wikipedia.org/wiki/Gene_knockout`, 2017.

[91] Wikipedia. Generalized extreme value distribution, — Wikipedia, the free encyclopedia. `Generalizedextremevaluedistribution`, 2017.

[92] Wikipedia. Giesecke & devrient, — Wikipedia, the free encyclopedia. `https://en.wikipedia.org/wiki/Giesecke_%26_Devrient`, 2017.

[93] Wikipedia. Girocard, — Wikipedia, the free encyclopedia. `https://en.wikipedia.org/wiki/Girocard`, 2017.

[94] Wikipedia. Goodness of fit, — Wikipedia, the free encyclopedia. `https://en.wikipedia.org/wiki/Goodness_of_fit`, 2017.

[95] Wikipedia. ideal, — Wikipedia, the free encyclopedia. `https://en.wikipedia.org/wiki/IDEAL`, 2017.

[96] Wikipedia. Imputation, — Wikipedia, the free encyclopedia. `https://en.wikipedia.org/wiki/Imputation_(statistics)`, 2017.

[97] Wikipedia. Information gain, — Wikipedia, the free encyclopedia. `https://en.wikipedia.org/wiki/Information_gain_ratio`, 2017.

[98] Wikipedia. Jcb, — Wikipedia, the free encyclopedia. `https://en.wikipedia.org/wiki/JCB_Co.,_Ltd`, 2017.

[99] Wikipedia. List of data breaches, — Wikipedia, the free encyclopedia. https://en.wikipedia.org/wiki/List_of_data_breaches, 2017.

[100] Wikipedia. Litecoin, — Wikipedia, the free encyclopedia. https://en.wikipedia.org/wiki/Litecoin, 2017.

[101] Wikipedia. Mastercard, — Wikipedia, the free encyclopedia. https://en.wikipedia.org/wiki/MasterCard, 2017.

[102] Wikipedia. Mean, — Wikipedia, the free encyclopedia. https://en.wikipedia.org/wiki/Mean, 2017.

[103] Wikipedia. Median, — Wikipedia, the free encyclopedia. https://en.wikipedia.org/wiki/Median, 2017.

[104] Wikipedia. Missing data, — Wikipedia, the free encyclopedia. https://en.wikipedia.org/wiki/Missing_data, 2017.

[105] Wikipedia. Money mule - — Wikipedia, the free encyclopedia. https://en.wikipedia.org/wiki/Money_mule, 2017.

[106] Wikipedia. Multicollinearity, — Wikipedia, the free encyclopedia. https://en.wikipedia.org/wiki/Multicollinearity, 2017.

[107] Wikipedia. Net promoter score, — Wikipedia, the free encyclopedia. https://en.wikipedia.org/wiki/Net_Promoter, 2017.

[108] Wikipedia. Normal distribution, — Wikipedia, the free encyclopedia. https://en.wikipedia.org/wiki/Normal_distribution, 2017.

[109] Wikipedia. Oberthur technologies, — Wikipedia, the free encyclopedia. https://en.wikipedia.org/wiki/Oberthur_Technologies, 2017.

[110] Wikipedia. Optical character recognition, — Wikipedia, the free encyclopedia. https://en.wikipedia.org/wiki/Optical_character_recognition, 2017.

[111] Wikipedia. Ownership, — Wikipedia, the free encyclopedia. https://en.wikipedia.org/wiki/Ownership, 2017.

[112] Wikipedia. Paypal, — Wikipedia, the free encyclopedia. https://en.wikipedia.org/wiki/PayPal, 2017.

[113] Wikipedia. Peercoin, — Wikipedia, the free encyclopedia. https://en.wikipedia.org/wiki/Peercoin, 2017.

[114] Wikipedia. Perfect plastic. http://perfectplastic.com/, 2017.

[115] Wikipedia. Phishing, — Wikipedia, the free encyclopedia. https://en.wikipedia.org/wiki/Phishing, 2017.

[116] Wikipedia. Plug-in, — Wikipedia, the free encyclopedia. https://en.wikipedia.org/wiki/Plug-in_(computing), 2017.

[117] Wikipedia. Principal component analysis, — Wikipedia, the free encyclopedia. https://en.wikipedia.org/wiki/Principal_component_analysis, 2017.

[118] Wikipedia. Projection, — Wikipedia, the free encyclopedia. https://en.wikipedia.org/wiki/Projection_(linear_algebra), 2017.

[119] Wikipedia. Receiver operating characteristics. https://en.wikipedia.org/wiki/Receiver_operating_characteristic#Area_under_the_curve, 2017.

[120] Wikipedia. Regularization (mathematics), — Wikipedia, the free encyclopedia. https://en.wikipedia.org/wiki/Regularization_(mathematics), 2017.

[121] Wikipedia. Rupay, — Wikipedia, the free encyclopedia. https://en.wikipedia.org/wiki/RuPay, 2017.

[122] Wikipedia. Single euro payments area, — Wikipedia, the free encyclopedia. (https://en.wikipedia.org/wiki/Single_Euro_Payments_Area), 2017.

[123] Wikipedia. Social engineering (security), — Wikipedia, the free encyclopedia. https://en.wikipedia.org/wiki/Social_engineering_(security), 2017.

[124] Wikipedia. Sparse matrix, — Wikipedia, the free encyclopedia. https://en.wikipedia.org/wiki/Sparse_matrix, 2017.

[125] Wikipedia. Statistical tests, — Wikipedia, the free encyclopedia. `https://en.wikipedia.org/wiki/Statistical_hypothesis_testing`, 2017.

[126] Wikipedia. Target now says 70 million people hit in data breach, the wall street journal, january 10, 2014. `https://www.wsj.com/articles/SB10001424052702303754404579312232546392464`, 2017.

[127] Wikipedia. Tf-idf, — Wikipedia, the free encyclopedia. `https://en.wikipedia.org/wiki/Tf%E2%80%93idf`, 2017.

[128] Wikipedia. Type i and type ii errors, — Wikipedia, the free encyclopedia. `https://en.wikipedia.org/wiki/Type_I_and_type_II_errors`, 2017.

[129] Wikipedia. Value at risk, — Wikipedia, the free encyclopedia. `https://en.wikipedia.org/wiki/Value_at_risk`, 2017.

[130] Wikipedia. Variable, — Wikipedia, the free encyclopedia. `https://en.wikipedia.org/wiki/Variable_(mathematics)`, 2017.

[131] Wikipedia. Vector space, — Wikipedia, the free encyclopedia. `https://en.wikipedia.org/wiki/Dimension_(vector_space)`, 2017.

[132] Wikipedia. Visa, inc., — Wikipedia, the free encyclopedia. `https://en.wikipedia.org/wiki/Visa_Inc.`, 2017.

[133] Wikipedia. Yahoo discloses new breach of 1 billion user accounts, new york times, december 15, 2016. `https://www.wsj.com/articles/yahoo-discloses-new-breach-of-1-billion-user-accounts-1481753131`, 2017.

[134] Wikipedia. Yodlee, — Wikipedia, the free encyclopedia. `https://en.wikipedia.org/wiki/Yodlee`, 2017.

Copyright notices

About the author

Fabrice Colas is a scientist, an entrepreneur, and a software engineer who studied in France (Eng. & M.Sc. research) and received a PhD in statistical learning from the Netherlands.

For several years, he worked as a postdoctoral scholar in human genetics and statistics in the United States and the Netherlands. Then he seized an opportunity at an international e-merchant to apply his knowledge towards reducing payment fraud.

Today, he helps businesses throughout Europe to reduce their exposure to financial and operational risks with risk management intelligence.

After spending ten years working throughout Europe, North America, and South America, Fabrice has obtained extensive experience in multiple cultures and languages. He focuses on empowering the businesses he works for and the people he works with.

in https://www.linkedin.com/in/fabricecolas/

www.ingramcontent.com/pod-product-compliance
Lightning Source LLC
LaVergne TN
LVHW022307060326
832902LV00020B/3326